HOW TO DOWNLOAD THE WALKING EYE APP

Available on purchase of this guide only.

1. Visit our website: www.insightguides.com/walkingeye
2. Download the Walking Eye container app to your smartphone (this will give you access to your free eBook and the ability to purchase other products)
3. Select the scanning module in the Walking Eye container app
4. Scan the QR Code on this page – you will be asked to enter a verification word from the book as proof of purchase
5. Download your free eBook* for travel information on the go

* Other destination apps and eBooks are available for purchase separately or are free with the purchase of the Insight Guide book

CONTENTS

ART & ARCHITECTURE

Whether it's ancient Vietnamese temples, Chinese shop houses or French colonial villas, great architecture is everywhere, from HCMC (route 1) and Hoi An Old Town (route 8) to Hanoi (route 12).

RECOMMENDED ROUTES FOR...

BEACHCOMBING

Vietnam's coastline is extensive, and while most cities on travellers' itineraries have a beachfront, routes 4 and 5 offer visitors the best of Vietnam's sunbathing and water sports.

CHAMPA KINGDOM

The Champa Kingdom controlled all of central Vietnam for over a century. Explore their temple ruins, ancient citadels, refined sculptures and thriving modern culture on routes 4 and 9.

CUISINE

Vietnamese cuisine is deservedly the subject of much international attention. Be sure to visit Hanoi (routes 12 and 13), Hue (route 10) and HCMC (routes 1 and 2) for the best selection of cuisine.

HILL TRIBES

Vietnam has a vast, mountainous interior inhabited by 54 recognised ethnic minorities. Meet some of them and learn about their traditional lifestyles on routes 6, 7 and 15.

MODERN VIETNAM

Vietnam has undergone a tremendous growth spurt over the last decade. Partake in urban Vietnam's nightlife, shopping and entertainment in HCMC (routes 1 and 2), Hanoi (routes 12 and 13) and Nha Trang (route 5).

OUTDOORS

Ecotourism is the least developed aspect of Vietnam's tourism industry, which is a surprise given its beautiful landscapes. Get your fill of the country's natural splendours on routes 7, 14, 15 and 16.

WAR HISTORY

Vietnam has been caught up in conflict during most of the nation's history. The last war with America is still the one on most people's minds. Get a glimpse into the past on routes 1, 2 and 13.

INTRODUCTION

An introduction to Vietnam's geography, customs and culture, plus illuminating background information on cuisine, history and what to do when you're there.

Tran Quoc Pagoda in Hanoi

EXPLORE VIETNAM

21st-century Vietnam is thriving economically and as a tourist destination thanks to freedoms introduced over the past three decades. Visitors are flocking here to explore the country's infamous history, diverse culture and modern dynamism.

Modern yet traditional, communist yet capitalist, cosmopolitan yet quaint – calling Vietnam diverse doesn't even begin to tell the story. Its associations with war may still be present, but today the tunnels are tourist traps, the tanks are displayed in museums and the divisions are all but healed.

The sheer range of landscapes and attractions makes Vietnam something of a challenge. The long, sandy beaches and the turquoise seas are tempting, but then so are its forested mountains and verdant countryside. Vietnamese cities are dynamic, full of life and colour. Today's ruling communist government still keeps a tight reign on cultural and political affairs, and the sheer pace of development means major cities are packed to bursting point. Despite this, there has never been a better time to visit Vietnam as much of the progress is aimed at attracting tourism. In the three decades since Vietnam first began to open up to the outside world, great changes have been made. Standards of living have risen dramatically, communications have improved and most of the country is now accessible.

The result is that travelling is simpler, the hotels are more luxurious and the restaurants of higher quality than ever before. Vietnam doesn't forget its past – that's why many visitors come, after all – but it is keen to move forward and showcase its natural beauty. And as a people, the Vietnamese are incredibly open, friendly and often eager to meet foreign travellers.

A DISTINCT IDENTITY

For more than 2,000 years Vietnam's development as a nation has been marked by its proximity to China. No country in Southeast Asia has spent so long fighting off Chinese domination. Likewise, the Vietnamese spent more than a millennium pushing against the Champa Kingdom to the south, until it was finally dissolved and its territory taken over by Emperor Minh Mang in the early 1800s.

There is a modern slogan: *Vietnam is a country, not a war*. However, for 35 years after World War II, Vietnam was almost synonymous with war, first with the French, then the Americans, and finally the Khmer Rouge, with Chinese reprisals. Perhaps because of the long years of rivalries, Vietnam has

Countryside around the village of Kenh Ga

developed a powerful sense of national identity, possessing a unique cultural heritage that is both strongly Sinicised and also distinctively Southeast Asian.

GEOGRAPHY AND LAYOUT

Northern Vietnam is anchored by Hanoi, an ancient city established 1,000 years ago. Beyond Hanoi, the provinces of the vast Red River Delta reflect the traditional agricultural culture on which the economy is based. The surrounding mountain regions, populated by hill tribes, ascend towards Laos in the west and north towards China.

Southwards, following the historical movement of the Viet people, is a chain of coastal provinces washed by the South China Sea. In the centre is Hue, the old imperial city of the Nguyen Dynasty, and vestiges of the Cham holy land at My Son.

In the south, the former capital of Saigon, now known as Ho Chi Minh City (HCMC), remains the country's economic and pop culture capital, and gateway to the Mekong. If Hanoi is a city of earth tones, Ho Chi Minh is neon, all lit up in lights.

Getting around Vietnam is becoming much easier with improved roads, airports and a reliable rail system which is now possible to book online. Still, neither Hanoi nor Ho Chi Minh City offers a viable mass urban transport system for visitors, and in both cities the best bet is to taxi from place to place. However, with a subway being built in Saigon and a sky train taking shape in Hanoi, this looks set to change.

HISTORICAL ARCHITECTURE

A curious blend of Chinese and French styles has influenced architecture in Hanoi, most of which dates from the last two centuries; there are some particularly great examples of colonial style in the French Quarter, while the city's temples and pagodas display the melding of Sino-Vietnamese design elements. Soviet brutalism can also be found here, while modern architecture is alive and well in the form of the skyscrapers now rising around town.

In the ancient port town of Hoi An visitors will find a blend of Chinese, Japanese and French influences, creating a unique and cohesive architectural style. Further southwest in the mountain resort of Da Lat an abundance of French colonial architecture has been preserved due to the absence of military action there during the Indochina wars.

The assimilation of external historical elements in Ho Chi Minh City has resulted in Vietnamese, Soviet, French, Western and Chinese architectural influences and a contrasting mishmash of edifices. Like in Hanoi, French colonial is still the city's loveliest architectural legacy, remaining highly visible today, although more and more examples are falling victim to the wrecking ball.

Beautiful Bai Sao Beach on Phu Quoc island

POPULATION

About 86 percent of Vietnam's population are ethnic Viets, also known as Kinh. They originated in southern China, where com-munities persist in an ancient culture and lifestyle. The remaining 14 percent of the population are officially divided among 54 ethnic groups, although in reality there are probably hundreds of different groups.

DON'T LEAVE VIETNAM WITHOUT...

Sipping a sundowner in Hanoi. As the sun sets in Hanoi, make your way to the Summit Lounge atop the Sofitel Plaza for knockout views across Truc Bach and West Lake.

Trekking around Sa Pa. In the far north, the majesty of the mountains is elevated by the colours of the hill peoples who call them home. Take a trek from Sa Pa itself or, even better, head out to the Topas Ecolodge, located 20km (12.4 miles) from town, and enjoy the mountain air away from the crowds.

Seeing Hoi An before the crowds. The Old Town of Hoi An is almost impossibly pretty and as a result it attracts hordes of tourists, so beat the masses and see the old streets populated by just the locals with a pre-breakfast amble.

Visiting the War Remnants Museum. It's a hard hitting place to visit, but to get a handle on what Vietnam has been through in terms of conflict, this Ho Chi Minh City museum is a must.

Eating my quang and cau lau. In Da Nang seek out a bowl of *my quang* and in Hoi An don't miss the local speciality of *cau lau* – two of the country's finest street food classics.

Strolling around Hoan Kiem. In the early morning or evening, Hoan Kiem Lake in Hanoi is thronged with walkers young and old, while games of street badminton strike up and laughing yoga groups come out in force. Be sure to get amongst it for a true taste of capital life.

Cruising Halong Bay. Set sail among the thousands of limestone outcrops that rear up from the emerald waters of Halong Bay on a traditional wooden junk. Enjoy a night on board under the stars and a sunrise tai chi session on deck.

Seeing sunset on the Mui Ne dunes. The Sahara-like red sand dunes of Mui Ne take on an extra level of magic come sundown, when the hue of the sand becomes more intense the deeper the sun dips, providing some of the best photo opportunities in the land.

Discovering the Delta's floating markets. Explore the working waters of the Mekong Delta by boat and see the flurry of activity at the morning floating markets. Get out as early as possible (at least before 8am) to see the best of the action.

Exploring royal tombs. Spend a day around the imperial city of Hue soaking in the grandeur of the royal mausoleums before enjoying the city's famed cuisine, which was created for the palates of past emperors.

Lang Son in the northeast

Vietnam's 1 million ethnic Chinese (Hoa) constitute the most important ethnic minority. The ancestors of the Hoa came principally from the southern Chinese provinces of Guangxi, Guangdong, Fujian, Zhejiang and Taiwan.

The Cham inhabit Ninh Thuan and Binh Thuan Province (the former Cham province of Panduranga), as well as parts of the Mekong Delta (and eastern Cambodia). Once masters of much of central Vietnam and portions of Cambodia and Laos, they now number around 150,000 within Vietnam. The coastal Cham are predominantly Hindu (Balamon), while those of the Mekong Delta are Muslim (Bani).

Ethnic minorities in the mountains of central Vietnam form another significant group. Called *montagnards* by the French, they include Muong, Ma, K'ho, Ede, Jarai, Bahnar and Sedang. The highlands of the north are home to numerous minorities as well, including the Tay, Tai, Hmong, Dao and Nung.

CITY LIFE

Living in cramped houses filled with extended three-generation families means that life often spills onto the streets. Itinerant vendors on bicycles and on foot, streetside barbers, shoeshine boys, not to mention the constant and chaotic flow of traffic, will assail your senses. Even in quieter residential areas, families often gather in the lanes to gossip with neighbours or buy fruit from passing vendors.

With a lot more cars, motorbikes and people than ever before, Vietnam's major cities suffer from chronic congestion, leading the government to impose restrictions on street activity. Street vendors, shopkeepers and food stalls are perpetually playing hide and seek with local police and district authorities who will confiscate goods – plastic stools, baskets, whatever – if these items are deemed to be blocking traffic or pushing pedestrians onto the road.

Vietnamese people of all ages love to *di choi* (go out to play). This means going out to have fun, hanging out with friends at a bar or café, singing karaoke, etc. When Vietnamese *di choi*, it's often a case of the more the merrier.

CLIMATE

The south has two seasons – wet and dry. The rains arrive in mid-May and leave in mid-December. Between these months it may rain fiercely for about one hour a day, normally in the afternoon or early evening. Late February to late April are the hottest months, with temperatures well into the mid-30s°C (86°F).

Central Vietnam from Da Nang to Nha Trang has its own weather patterns due to the monsoons: the dry season is from January to September, with the rainfall from October to mid-January. The seasons are not as pronounced here, however, and it can rain at any time of the year. Hue, the wettest city in Vietnam, as well as the

Evidence of higher disposable incomes

Western Highlands, tends to get a lot of rain throughout the year.

The north experiences four seasons. The summer months from May to September are almost always hot and humid, with the most rainfall during this period. Winter, from late December to early March, is often grey, drizzly and cool, but these months can also bring spells of brilliant clear and crisp weather, especially in the mountains

LOCAL CUSTOMS

Most banks, public services and state-run offices work Monday to Friday, opening between 7.30 and 8.30am, and closing between 4 and 5pm, with a lunch break between 11.30 and 1.30. Museums roughly follow the same hours, but generally close on Monday. Tourist-orientated shops work a seven-day week from 8am to 9pm. Markets open as early as 5.30am, winding down by lunchtime. Only very large markets in city centres stay active all day.

Tourists staying in hotels and guesthouses do not need to register with the police directly. When you check in at reception the staff will take your passport for registration. They will return it to you the next morning.

POLITICS AND ECONOMY

The Socialist Republic of Vietnam (the country's full title) is a one-party communist state. The 1986 Doi Moi (Reno-vation) policies initiated a move toward a 'socialist-oriented market economy' but did little to shake up the monopoly on ideology and power of the leadership in charge. However, there has been a vast economic revolution and speedy national development with the advent (as yet incomplete) of privatisation. Foreign investment is key to Vietnam's growing economy with, ironically, the United States now taking the lead as Vietnam's largest business and trade partner.

The economic impact of Viet Kieu (overseas Vietnamese) cannot be understated. Many fleed the country as refugees after the fall of Saigon, then resettled in Western countries (particularly the United States and Australia) and began sending money to their relatives left behind in Vietnam. These remittances are now estimated to average an astounding US$7 billion per year. Realising the danger of losing this revenue as the Viet Kieu age, the government has begun relaxing punitive regulations and encouraging Viet Kieu to return, invest and retire here.

Social reforms, though not tied to Doi Moi, have increased, bringing a wide array of new freedoms in the spheres of religion, art and communications. Access to the internet, cable television, the availability of Western films and music, and the influx of foreign tourists and expatriates have only accelerated this influence of Western culture and continued the trend toward expanded social freedoms.

Hanoi's Old East Gate *Diamond Plaza shopping centre, HCMC*

TOP TIPS FOR VISITING VIETNAM

When to visit. Determining the 'best time to visit Vietnam' is entirely subjective, since each region has its own weather patterns. Furthermore, the rainy season is not necessarily a bad time to visit, as showers are usually a brief afternoon interlude, and can be planned around. The rains have the added benefit of cooling the temperatures and initiating the growth of foliage and flora.

Safe street food. When eating street food and at small canteens and diners, try to select a venue that is crowded. This not only suggests that the food tastes good, but is also fresh.

Water and ice. It is safest only to drink bottled water, soft drinks or boiled beverages (tea and coffee). Ice is generally safe; however, if it is being hacked off a block on the pavement, it is best avoided!

Sun care. Bring your own high factor sunscreen from home as many of the creams on sale in Vietnam double as skin whitening agents.

Plan ahead. Be sure to buy advanced tickets for the evening performance of Hanoi's Thang Long Water Puppet Theatre first thing in the morning or the day before, as they tend to sell out, especially at weekends.

Stay warm. Sa Pa and the Northern Highlands is the coldest region in Vietnam. Especially when visiting in winter months, be sure to pack some warm clothing. Be aware that many budget hotels and restaurants do not have heating and it gets quite chilly at night.

Visas. Be sure to check the current visa situation well in advance and arrange your visa letter through an agent if required.

Copy your passport. In Vietnam it is handy to have a photocopy of your passport to hand in on check in at hotels if you want to keep your original copy on your person.

Learn from a local. Vietnamese people love it when visitors speak even the smallest amount of their language, so ask the hotel staff how to say hello and thank you – trying to learn the language from a book without pronunciation help is an uphill battle!

Rise early. Vietnamese people rise early and to see the best of most places, the earlier you can get up, the better.

Slow down. The Vietnamese, especially outside of HCMC, like to take their time over a coffee to chat and watch the world go by. Be sure to leave some time in your own schedule to do the same.

Drink bia hoi. In Hanoi don't miss the chance to drink the cheapest beer of your life at a pavement side bia hoi. Be sure to order some food to go with it.

Carry small notes. For taxis, buying water on the street and other small transactions, a few 10,000 dong notes will be much better than a fistful of 500,000s.

Rainy season footwear. If you are in Vietnam in the rainy season, consider wearing open sandals or flip flops to let the water out if you're caught in a downpour.

Rau thom, a platter of raw herbs served as an accompaniment to the meal

FOOD AND DRINK

The essence of Vietnamese cuisine is the pursuit of perfect harmony and balance among the five flavours: sweet, sour, savoury, spicy and bitter. This balance may be achieved in a single dish or through a banquet, but the experience is always memorable.

Vietnamese cuisine is light, delicious, generally very healthy, and comes in endless variety. Rice *(com)* is the staple, topped with meat, fish and vegetables. Many Vietnamese believe that a proper meal must always include rice. Thus, one of the most common questions in Vietnamese following a greeting is, *'An com chua?'* (Have you eaten rice yet?). Fresh, raw herbs, subtly spicy broths, separate dipping sauces, and condiments are prevalent in Vietnamese cuisine. Most sauces are made with a base of *nuoc mam* (a pungent fish sauce).

Modern Vietnamese cuisine borrows heavily from Chinese, but also has significant influence from French, and some elements introduced by Portuguese, Khmer and indigenous Cham. The Chinese contributed stir-fries, spring rolls, noodles and soy sauce; the French brought baguettes, pastries, pâté and dairy products. Together with the Portuguese, the French also introduced many of Vietnam's staples, including coffee, black pepper, potatoes and tapioca. Curries and many other spices probably came to Vietnam through the Cham and Khmer (both heavily influenced by Indian culture themselves).

LOCAL CUISINES

Vietnam has three main culinary regions: the north (including Hanoi), the south (including HCMC) and the centre (including Da Nang Hue and Hoi An), each with differences in both their main dishes and snacks, as well as their use of ingredients and methods of cooking.

The unofficial national dish, *pho* (rice noodle soup) is the most common street food, especially in Hanoi. Usually eaten for breakfast, it makes a tasty meal at any time of the day. A hot, aromatic broth is poured over noodles topped with either slivers of beef *(bo)* or chicken *(ga)* to which diners add their own chillies, lime and sauces. In the south a huge plate of herbs accompanies each bowl. A Hanoi favourite is *bun cha*, charcoal-grilled pork meatballs served in a light broth, accompanied by cold vermicelli noodles, lettuce and herbs.

Based on literary accounts, *pho* surfaced sometime after the French occupation of Hanoi in the mid-1880s. While its roots remain the subject of debate, there is compelling evidence that it sprang from an unlikely marriage of Chinese and French culinary influences. It

Hoi An cuisine

is said the French popularised the use of bones and lesser cuts of beef to make the broth, which forms the base of the soup. Some say that *pho* was devised by Vietnamese who learned to make *pot-au-feu* for their French employers. The theory goes that the name actually comes from the French *feu*.

Hue, a city associated with Buddhism, is famous for its vegetarian cuisine as well as the food of the royal court. As the seat of Vietnam's last royal dynasty, many of the local dishes were once reserved only for the king. Typical Hue specialities include *bun bo* – fried beef and noodles served with coriander, onion, garlic, cucumber, chilli peppers and tomato paste – as well as *banh khoai*, a potato pancake.

As the country's modern commercial capital, Ho Chi Minh City is a place where food from every region can be found in bountiful supply. One of the city's most celebrated local dishes is *banh xeo*, a sizzling crêpe pan-fried with pork, shrimps and bean sprouts, which is folded over and cooked to a crispy golden brown. Other popular Vietnamese dishes include *cha gio*: 'spring rolls' of minced pork, prawn, crabmeat, mushrooms and vegetables wrapped in thin rice paper and then deep-fried. These are then rolled in a lettuce leaf with fresh mint and other herbs, and dipped in a sweet fish sauce known as *nuoc cham*.

The other great Vietnamese staple is *nuoc mam* (fish sauce) which is used as an ingredient as well as a dipping sauce for dishes such as spring rolls or *banh*

xeo pancakes. *Nuoc mam* has a pungent aroma and biting saltiness that is an acquired taste, but it's the perfect complement to the subtle flavours of the food. Produced in coastal cities such as Phan Thiet and Phu Quoc, fish sauce is made by fermenting anchovies and salt in large wooden barrels for about six months.

WHERE TO EAT

Street food

The most authentic (and best) Vietnamese food is found along street sides, down alleys and inside local markets, where stall keepers specialise in just one dish and serve the freshest food. Look out for signs over stalls with steaming cauldrons surrounded by toy-sized plastic chairs. Try to arrive in local street-food eateries before 9am for breakfast, by noon for lunch and 6–7pm for dinner, as food can run out early. Compared to other countries, it's still relatively inexpensive in Vietnam to dine out, and street food is astoundingly good value. Expect to pay from $1–2 per person on the street.

Roadside shacks are found in almost every town and offer quick and simple dishes – a bowl of steaming noodles or a beef stew filled with vegetables. Also ubiquitous are sliced and diced pineapples, mangos and guavas. For those who just want a drink, Vietnam's café culture extends to the street: pull up a stool and wait for the thick, rich coffee to come. For those who want something more filling, the list of options is immense.

Baguettes for sale – a sign of the country's former colonial past

Most vendors have the names of their wares printed on their carts. Among the most popular options are bite-size snacks that are deep-fried or grilled. The nation's favourite noodles, *pho*, or snacks such as *ca vien* (fish balls on a stick) are packed with flavour.

Each region has its own culinary quirk. In the north, dishes such as *bun cha*, sliced pork with vermicelli, are famous. In the central provinces, the best-known snack is *banh bao*, a soft, dumpling-like creation. Down south, the use of coconut milk and lime juice is more in evidence. Hu tieu mi, a mass of noodles and vegetables, is a classic southern dish, as is *banh bot chien* (nothing to do with dogs!), a fried rice-flour cake.

Street food is generally safe to eat, but the normal rules apply: go for ice cubes, not the crushed variety, and remember that fruits you can peel have been less exposed to germs than those that have been laid out in the open for hours.

Diners and canteens

Basic indoor eateries, sometimes served out of homes or shops, normally offer only one or two house specialities – noodle soups or rice meals with a selection of meat and vegetables. The differences from street food are found in the slightly higher prices, better seating arrangements and more reliable opening hours. Usually diners and canteens are open for breakfast and dinner, but most are closed for lunch, as Vietnamese tend to go home during their lunch hour. The

exceptions are takeaways serving *com binh danh* – rice buffets. Sometimes the selection in the morning is different from the evening offering at any given venue. Canteens usually have no menus, and often no beverages other than iced tea and cola.

Vietnamese restaurants

Typical Vietnamese restaurants have a party atmosphere and are indeed popular for special occasions. The setting is open-air with long tables and chairs. Menus offer a large variety of meat and seafood dishes. Vegetarian options are sparse. *Lau* (hotpot eaten family-style) is the most popular dish in these restaurants. Beer is the beverage of choice alongside vodka.

Foreign restaurants

Foreign-owned restaurants and Vietnamese-owned restaurants serving foreign food are becoming ever more common, serving both locals and expats. The quality and variety of foreign food has vastly improved in Vietnam over the last decade, and now cuisines from France, Italy, India, Germany, the UK, the Middle East and North America are well represented. Standards range from backpacker lounges to fine, classical French dining.

Fast food and foreign coffee

Fast food arrived in Vietnam much later than surrounding countries. A few Western-style fast-food chains and cafes, like Lotteria (a Korean counterpart to McDon-

Banh xeo, a Vietnamese crêpe

Bonsai dinner cruise in HCMC

alds), Kentucky Fried Chicken and Highlands Coffee (the Vietnamese answer to Starbucks) have been around for a while. Thankfully the local Vietnamese cafe culture is proving robust.

DRINKS

Fruit shakes

Vietnam cultivates a multitude of tropical fruits such as mango, custard apple, durian, pineapple, star fruit, rambutan and dragon fruit. Many are grown in the Mekong Delta and Da Lat, Vietnam's market garden centre. Found everywhere are *sinh to* stalls, recognisable by their glass cases displaying a variety of fruits and a few vegetables. Point to a selection of fruit and you will receive a thick shake, mixed with sugar *(duong)*, ice and condensed milk.

Coffee and tea

The Vietnamese love their coffee. Vietnam is the world's second-largest coffee exporter after Brazil, and domestic coffee is decent and strong. Most coffee is grown in the Central Highlands, in the vicinity of Buon Ma Thuot. Coffee *(ca phe)* comes iced *(da)* or hot *(nong)*; in local establishments, milk *(sua)* is usually sweetened and condensed. The Vietnamese prefer green tea to black, which is grown in the Central and Northern Highlands.

Wine

Grapes are grown mostly in Ninh Thuan Province, and then processed in Da Lat.

Da Lat wine comes in red and white, but neither are particularly palatable. Thankfully, better restaurants have a large imported selection.

Rice wine

Rice wine comes in three main varieties: plain distilled alcohol known as *ruou gao*, 'medicinal' distilled alcohol infused with plants and whole animals *(ruou thuoc)*, and ruou can, which is a sweet alcohol fermented in large ceramic jars by hill tribes who drink it on special occasions, through long bamboo straws.

Beer

The Vietnamese are avid beer-drinkers. Saigon Beer is the popular and inexpensive local brand, with both red and green labels. Bia Hanoi and Hanoi Beer are also big sellers in the north, while Larue and Huda are the biggest names in central Vietnam. Tiger and Heineken are also readily available. *Bia hoi*, or fresh (and very cheap) beer, is particularly popular in Hanoi. Places with a wider selection of imported beers are often called 'Beer Clubs'.

Food and drink prices

Cost of a meal for one including up to three dishes and a drink:
$$$$ = over US$15
$$$ = US$10–15
$$ = US$5–10
$ = under US$5

SHOPPING

Vietnam's markets are a highlight of any visit. The settings are as diverse as the goods on offer, whether paddling through Mekong floating markets, buying hill–tribe textiles right from the loom or procuring brand names at high–rise malls.

The biggest recent changes in Vietnam's shopping scene have been the creation of new, home-grown designer brands as well as a trend towards high-rise, luxury shopping malls. Stricter laws on copyright have also meant a modest reduction, but not elimination, of counterfeiting.

SHOPPING AREAS

Hanoi
For those with money to burn and space in their suitcases, Hanoi can be a shopper's paradise. Exquisite silks, colourful lacquerware, gems, silver, water puppets, scarves, fake war mementoes and hand-tailored clothing can all be found at reasonable prices within the city centre. In the Old Quarter, Hang Gai (Silk Street) has a clutch of top-notch silk shops, while Nha Tho Street offers some of the best clothing, handbags and home-decor items. In the city's bright, air-conditioned malls, shops selling brand-name electronics, clothing and cosmetics do a booming business thanks to a new generation of affluent Vietnamese consumers.

Hoi An
Hoi An's Old Town has some of the best shopping in Vietnam. For many years Hoi An has been known as the centre of silk fabric and tailor shops, many of which are housed in the old Chinese merchant shop houses. While tailoring is key to Hoi An's economy, in recent years an increasing number of souvenir shops have joined the commercial fray. Hoi An's Central Market is located across from the Quang Cong Temple at the end of Nguyen Hue Street. You will find even better bargains on souvenirs here than at the boutique shops in town. Keep in mind that tailoring a suit within 24 hours does not make for the ideal working conditions for those creating your outfit, nor does it allow for the highest quality workmanship.

Dalat
The Central Market in Dalat has a plethora of wares, from candied fruit and local wines to deer jerky and souvenirs. The three-storey structure (food on the middle floor, souvenirs and clothes above and below) dates from 1958 and is found at the junction of Nguyen Thi Minh Khai and Le Dai Hanh. Dalat is famous for its roses and other flowers, sold

One of the two Ipa-Nima accessories shops in Hanoi

around the outside of the ground floor. Strawberries are abundant – candied, as syrup, turned to wine or blended in fresh strawberry milkshakes. Artichokes are grown here and made into tea called tra atiso or actiso. You may also want to try the locally-produced Vang Dalat, or Dalat wine. XQ Historical Village is a must-visit for silk embroidery.

Ho Chi Minh City

Shopping in HCMC has dramatically improved in recent years, and it is fast emerging as a key Asian shopping and design hub. Although still a source of cheap, mass-produced goods, Vietnam's undisputed shopping capital now offers stylish, home-grown stores selling contemporary stuff at down-to-earth prices. Local talent and HCMC-based international designers create exceptional home accessories, furniture, lighting, modern art and clothing. Many innovative designers combine ancient artisanal techniques with contemporary designs to create both decorative and practical goods.

Souvenirs like marble stone boxes, ceramic tea sets, silk lanterns and more are sold at the countless souvenir stores located along Dong Khoi and Le Loi streets, and around the backpacker area of De Tham and Pham Ngo Lao streets. Ben Thanh Market is the city's best-known covered market and sells piles of cheap and cheerful souvenirs and handicrafts (like lacquerware, ceramics, coffee beans, T-shirts, conical hats and more) in a relatively compact ground-floor area. At night it is also a very popular eating area, open late.

BARGAINING

Prices in Vietnam are usually negotiable, except in supermarkets where they are marked. When haggling, it is important to smile and remain polite. If a price seems high, counter-offer 50 percent and then negotiate to a happy medium. It's important not to fret too much over a few thousand dong. The most important principle in haggling is arriving at a price both parties are happy with, but not necessarily reaching the cheapest price possible.

What not to buy

Vietnam has very strict regulations on the sale and export of genuine antiques, and as such, most 'antique' art pieces sold to tourists are fakes or copies. If someone claims they are selling an original piece, ask to see a certificate of authenticity and ownership.

Vietnam now has strict laws prohibiting the sale of products made from endangered species and other wild animals, but there are still too many loopholes to exploit and many people who break the law outright. To be safe, don't buy insect or butterfly collections, snake wine, coral pieces, sea turtle shells, bear teeth or tiger claw necklaces. Unfortunately all are readily available, and usually come from wild, rather than captive-raised animals.

Water puppets

ENTERTAINMENT

Spend a night at the opera, an evening at a pavement side bia hoi, or enjoy dance at a Saigon club. Between traditional and contemporary culture, Vietnam offers entertainment for everyone from families to young backpackers.

While certainly much more active than neighbouring Cambodia or Laos, Vietnam's evening entertainment options are nonetheless a little subdued. Traditional entertainment, some of it refurbished for the tourism industry, includes water puppetry and costumed music shows. The most popular performance art throughout the country is what can best be described as classical folk opera.

Ho Chi Minh City is the centre of Vietnamese pop culture, and it is here that most of the country's music is produced. Likewise, many of the best bars, clubs and nightlife options are located here, although the number of live music venues and quality bars in Hanoi has grown significantly in the last few years.

THEATRE

Water puppetry, though a once-popular, ancient art form, is now almost exclusively performed for tourism, be it local or international. While it is showcased in Ho Chi Minh City and Hue, it is most popularly seen near its place of origin, in Hanoi (see page 89). Puppeteers perform in a chest-deep pool of water behind a curtain on stage. The puppets usually range from 30–100cm (12–39 inches) and weigh from 1–5kg (2–11lbs), though larger puppets can weigh up to 20kg (44lbs) and need four people to manipulate them.

Classical folk opera comes in many names and forms, including *Cheo, Boi, Tuong* and *Cai Luong*. It is a sincere and authentic art form of rural peasants, rather than the high court. Troupes of performers travel the countryside, performing in temples and local arts centers. However some theatres, such as Cheo Hanoi Theatre (see page 118), have regular shows. Unfortunately this art form appears to be dying out due to the new availability and immense popularity of cable television.

DANCE

Unlike neighbouring Cambodia, Vietnam does not have a refined classical dance tradition, although many of the minority groups have traditional dance forms that can be witnessed in shows arranged for visiting tourists.

At the bar in Hanoi's Funky Buddha

There are also classical ballet schools, however, which do occasionally perform at the opera houses in HCMC and Hanoi.

MUSIC

Love it or hate it, it's hard to escape Vietnamese pop music. Long influenced by American music, it is beginning to become overshadowed by the influx of Korean boy-bands that have overtaken much of Southeast Asian pop culture. Vietnamese pop singers, from superstars to lounge singers, all perform at venues in big cities called *Phong Tra Ca Nhac* (Music Tea Rooms), as well as fairgrounds in the provinces.

Many bars, restaurants and hotels catering to tourists now offer live music as well. In Hanoi and Saigon there are a number of music venues playing host to quality home-grown acts as well as the increasing number, albeit small number of international acts that include Vietnam on an Asian tour circuit. Jazz music has a small following in both Hanoi and HCMC.

FILM

There is no shortage of films about Vietnam, mostly from the American viewpoint of the war era. Notables include *The Deer Hunter* (1978), *Apocalypse Now* (1979), *Platoon* (1986), *Full Metal Jacket* (1987), *Good Morning, Vietnam* (1987), *The Scent of Green Papaya* (1993) and *The Beautiful Country* (2004). Though many travel documentaries have recently been filmed in Vietnam, few contemporary foreign films have shot in the country. The two most famous films are probably *Indochine* (1992) and *The Quiet American* (2002).

Domestic films have tended to focus on romantic comedies, Chinese mythology or revolutionary history (all, of course, pro-communist). The local film industry was neither very serious nor taken seriously until a recent influx of Vietnamese-American actors joined the industry, including Johnny Tri Nguyen *(Spider-Man 2, X-Men: First Class)* and Dustin Nguyen *(21 Jump Street, Little Fish)*. The two appeared together in the groundbreaking Vietnamese film, *The Rebel* (2007).

Since 2008 there has been an explosion of Western-style cinemas in Vietnam.

NIGHTLIFE

Not unexpectedly, the centres of Vietnam's nightlife, in the form of popular bars and dance clubs, are HCMC and Hanoi, although Da Nang too now has a few options. HCMC has a growing crop of sky bars with awesome views of the city, while Hanoi has some laid back drinking holes and the more raucous bar strips that cluster around the bia hoi corner of Ta Hien street in the Old Quarter.

Leaving offerings at Tay Ho Pagoda

FESTIVALS

At times Vietnamese culture can look like one party after another. Whether it's the Lunar New Year, the Mid-Autumn Festival or Buddha's Birthday, there's a festival – or several festivals – to celebrate every month.

Vietnam has a vast number of traditional religious and cultural festivals. Some are celebrated across the country, but each province, and often each village or temple, may have its own unique calendar of events. All traditional festivals occur according to the lunar calendar (a gift from the Chinese); a few dates may be altered according to messages from sacred oracles (or the local People's Committee governing board).

Common elements in traditional festivals include temple visits, offerings to ancestors or tutelary gods, costumes, dragon and lion dancing, music, parades and lots of food.

JANUARY–FEBRUARY

Tet (first–third day of first lunar month). The biggest and most important celebration of the entire year, Tet Nguyen Dan (in full) heralds the start of the Vietnamese Lunar New Year. The most important days of Tet ('festival') are the first three days of the Lunar New Year. However, the holiday ceremonially lasts for two weeks. Either way the whole country shuts down for about a week. Everyone returns home for the holidays, including many overseas Vietnamese. The most interesting time for visitors is actually the week prior to the holiday, when night markets are a commotion of candy, flower and lantern vendors. Tet eve is celebrated with fireworks and dragon and lion dancing.

Hai Ba Trung Festival (sixth day of the second lunar month). This festival is held in Hanoi, at the Hai Ba Trung Temple. It honours the heroic resistance of the Trung sisters against the Chinese.

MARCH–APRIL

Perfume Pagoda Festival (15th day of the second lunar month). Thousands of Buddhist pilgrims flock to one of Vietnam's most revered pilgrimage sites, southwest of Hanoi (see route 14), to pray for good luck in the coming year.

Holiday of the Dead (fifth day of the third lunar month). On this day many people visit the graves of their ancestors to tend them and make offerings.

Elephant Race Festival (middle of

Tet celebrations in Hanoi

the third lunar month). Elephant races occur in Ban Don Village near Buon Ma Thuat, and they are a traditional event for the M'Nong tribe. Ethnic music, dancing and drinking of *ruou can* (bamboo pole wine) are all part of the festivities.

Thay Pagoda Festival (fifth–seventh day of the third lunar month). In celebration of the pagoda's revered Buddhist monk and puppeteer, the festivities include water puppetry and rowing contests.

MAY–JUNE

Phat Dan (eighth day of the fourth lunar month). Buddha's rites of passage are celebrated in pagodas, temples and homes, and sometimes with parades.

Tet Doan Ngo (Summer Solstice Day; fifth day of the fifth lunar month). This Tet includes festivities to ensure good health and well-being. Offerings are made to spirits, ghosts and the God of Death, to ward off summer epidemics.

Trang Nguyen (Wandering Souls Day; 15th day of the seventh lunar month). This is the second-most important Vietnamese festival. Graves are cleaned and offerings are made for the wandering souls of the forgotten dead.

Hue City Festival. This is a biennial celebration during even-numbered years, celebrating the Nguyen Dynasty and the cultural heritage of Hue.

Expect parades, lots of performers, games and numerous special events.

SEPTEMBER–OCTOBER

Tet Trung Thu (Mid-Autumn Festival; 15th day of the eighth lunar month). Children parade around with candle-illuminated lanterns, and delicious pastry-covered 'mooncakes' with sweet lotus-seed or red-bean paste are eaten.

Kate Festival (eighth or ninth lunar month). Getting the date right of this Cham festival (often mistakenly called the 'Cham New Year') is difficult because it falls within a unique Cham lunar calendar. It's usually early October. The festival is held at ancient Cham temples in Phan Thiet and Phan Rang, with feasting, music and processions.

Whale Festival (16th–18th day of the eighth lunar month). Known as both Lang Ca Ong and Cau Ngu, it is celebrated in Vung Tau and other southern fishing communities. In Phan Thiet it occurs in odd-numbered years. Festivities include parades with costumed performers, dragon and lion dances, and processions of whale bones.

NOVEMBER–DECEMBER

Da Lat Flower Festival. This is a week-long festival with parades, street food, games, live music, and endless flower markets and flower exhibits. Occasionally it may occur in January.

Sixteenth Century Portuguese map featuring Vietnam

HISTORY: KEY DATES

Wars, wars and more wars…despite a history of conflict for more than 1,000 years with the Chinese, Cham, French, Japanese, Cambodians and Americans, Vietnam's rich culture has flourished and evolved into a diverse but unified nation.

CHINA AND THE STRUGGLE FOR INDEPENDENCE

258BC	Thuc Pan establishes new Vietnamese state called Au Lac.
207BC	Trieu Da, renegade Chinese general, conquers Au Lac and establishes power over Nam Viet.
111BC	Heirs of Trieu Da submit to Han Chinese emperor.
AD40	Trung sisters lead first major rebellion against Chinese.
938	Ngo Quyen wins Bach Dang battle, ending 1,000 years of Chinese rule.
1516	Portuguese seafarers are first Westerners to arrive in Vietnam.
1539–1778	Trinh lords rule north, while Nguyen lords control south.

THE NGUYEN DYNASTY AND THE FRENCH

1802–19	Nguyen Anh defeats Tay Sons, proclaiming himself Emperor Gia Long.
1861	French forces capture Saigon.
1862	Tu Duc signs a compromising peace treaty with the French.
1883	France establishes protectorate, ruling Cochinchina as a colony.

COMMUNISM AND REBELLION

1930	Ho Chi Minh forms Vietnamese Communist Party.
1940	Japan occupies Vietnam, leaving French administration intact.
1945	Japan defeated; Ho Chi Minh declares independence and Vietnam a Democratic Republic.
1946	French bombard Haiphong. Viet Minh withdraws from Hanoi. First Indochina War begins.
1954	Battle of Dien Bien Phu. Geneva Accord divides Vietnam: south led by Catholic Ngo Dinh Diem, north by communist Ho Chi Minh.

North Vietnamese troops enter Saigon on tanks and trucks, ending the Vietnam War

WAR WITH USA

1955	Diem refuses to hold elections. Second Indochina War begins.
1960	North Vietnam introduces conscription. US advisers in South.
1965	US President Johnson commences bombing of North; first US combat troops land at Danang.
1968	US troops rise to 540,000, but Tet Offensive saps morale.
1969	Ho Chi Minh dies aged 79; US begins phased troops withdrawal.
1973	Washington and Hanoi sign ceasefire. Last US troops withdrawn.

REUNIFICATION

1975	NVA captures Saigon. Vietnam unified. US imposes trade embargo.
1976	Socialist Republic of Vietnam declared.
1978	Cambodian troops mount cross-border attacks into southern Vietnam. Vietnam invades Cambodia, overthrowing Khmer Rouge.
1979	China retaliates by invading northern Vietnam.

MODERNISATION

1986	6th Party Congress embraces Doi Moi (economic renovation).
1991	China relations normalised.
1994	US Trade Embargo lifted.
1995	Vietnam becomes official member of ASEAN (Association of Southeast Asian Nations).
2000	Bill Clinton becomes first US president to visit since the war.
2001	US–Vietnam Bilateral Trade Agreement signed.
2003	Vietnam hosts 22nd SEA Games.
2004	Hill Tribes Protest in Central Highlands, government cracks down.
2007	Vietnam joins World Trade Organization (WTO).
2010	US publicly sides with Vietnam against China in territorial dispute.
2011	Nguyen Phu Trong becomes General Secretary. Vietnam and China sign deal on South China Sea dispute.
2013	Vietnam signs UN Convention Against Torture and is elected to the UN Human Rights Council.
2014	Anti-China protests and riots following China's relocation of an oil rig to near the disputed Paracel islands.
2015	Vietnam signs TPP (Trans-Pacific Partnership).

BEST ROUTES

HCMC's skyline

HO CHI MINH CITY: THE QUIET AMERICAN TOUR

Relive Graham Greene's famous novel 'The Quiet American', right where he wrote it. However, modern Ho Chi Minh City is a world away from 1950s Saigon, so soak up the contrast of old and new in Vietnam's economic capital.

DISTANCE: 5.7km (3.5 miles)
TIME: A full-day walk through a bustling city
START: Hotel Majestic
END: Former American Legation at intersection of Ham Nghi and Ho Tung Mau streets
POINTS TO NOTE: This tour can easily be merged with route 2, as streets overlap. Transport by taxi and motorbike is available, as well as cyclo (though the latter is not recommended for safety).

Read *The Quiet American* before setting out. In the 1955 novel, Graham Greene's Fowler attempts to lay bare the bones of one of Saigon's most Machiavellian eras. Set in the twilight of French influence, the novel recalls a murky 'what might have been' scenario tracing the outset of US involvement in Vietnam. Greene's Saigon is filled with war correspondents, doomed innocents and glasses of vermouth cassis.

THE RIVERFRONT

Begin at the **Hotel Majestic** ❶ (1 Dong Khoi Street). Built by the French in 1925, this was one of South-east Asia's classic colonial hotels. The rooftop bar commands great views of the **Saigon River**. In the 1950s, covering the Franco-Viet Minh War, British war correspondent Graham Greene lived in Suite R404, where he wrote some of *The Quiet American*.

To your right lies the **Port of Saigon**, the largest port in Vietnam. The big salmon-pink building on the opposite side of the river is the old customs house, nicknamed 'Dragon House', and built by a French mercantile company in 1862. It was from here that Ho Chi Minh set off on his 30 years of travels.

DONG KHOI STREET

Turn left out of the Majestic and walk up **Dong Khoi Street** away from the river. In the early 1900s, this tree-lined boulevard was known as Rue Catinat, edged with fashionable boutiques, cafés and theatres. The epicentre of the original

Urban fashion for men and women at Mai's on Dong Khoi

French Quarter, the impressive edifices built along here by the colonials are today some of the city's key historical sights.

Dong Khoi is now the city's main tourism and commercial street, lined with fashionable boutiques, art galleries, souvenir shops, shopping plazas and five-star hotels. It offers broad choices in merchandise, including hill-tribe crafts, silk, lacquer and oil paintings, as well as imported brands like Calvin Klein, Gucci, Louis Vuitton and Versace.

Bisecting Dong Khoi is **Mac Thi Buoi Street**, previously Rue d'Ormay. This street housed one of the notorious opium dens that Greene's protagonist, Fowler, was so fond of. Today it also has many interesting boutiques.

LAM SON SQUARE

Continuing up Dong Khoi, you'll arrive at Lam Son Square, at the corner of Dong Khoi Street and Le Loi Boulevard. Formerly Place Garnier, this was the setting of General Thé's terrorist bombing in *The Quiet American*. Opposite on Dong Khoi was the Girval Café, where Greene's Phuong stopped for her 'elevenses', or for afternoon tea. The entire block is now home to a massive shopping centre.

On the northern side of the square, the colonial **Hotel Continental** ❷ no longer has the famous Continental Shelf Café, where Fowler sipped vermouth cassis. However, it retains the charming inner courtyard café. Graham

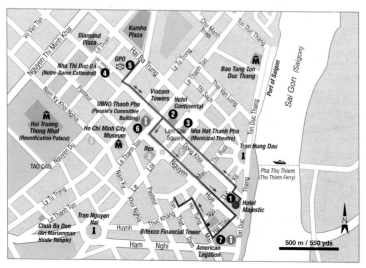

Municipal Theatre

Greene wrote much of *The Quiet Amer-ican* here, while residing in Room 214.

The neoclassical **Municipal Theatre ③** (Nha Hat Thanh Pho) stands sandwiched between the Continental, Park Hyatt Sai-gon and towering Caravelle Hotel. This former opera house hosts occasional classical music and dance performances, advertised by banners outside.

At this point a diversion to **L'Usine**, see ①, is in order for lunch. Backtrack to Doneg Khoi and locate L'Usine up a flight of stairs at the end of the art stall lined alleyway.

The Cao Dai Holy See

In the 1920s, Ngo Van Chieu formed the Cao Dai religion, following a revelation of 'The Way' in a dream. In 1926, one of his followers, Le Van Trung, deserted with 20,000 disciples, crowned himself pon-tiff and built the Cao Dai Temple at Tay Ninh, north of Saigon. Graham Greene described the temple as 'a Walt Disney fantasia of the East'. Seven years later, Le Van Trung was deposed for embez-zling the temple funds.

Cao Daism seeks to create the ulti-mate religion by fusing Buddhist, Tao-ist, Confucian and Catholic beliefs into a synthesis of its own. Today, around 3 million Vietnamese still follow the Cao Dai Way, although séances – which used to be held to contact 'saints' like Sun Yat Sen and Victor Hugo – are no longer practised.

NOTRE-DAME CATHEDRAL AND POST OFFICE

Continuing up Dong Khoi Street, you'll pass the sparkling **Vincom Towers**. This enormous shopping plaza is one of the largest in Vietnam. Straight ahead is **Notre-Dame Cathedral ④** (Nha Thi Duc Ba), described by Graham Greene as 'the hideous pink Cathedral' in the aftermath of the bombing at Place Garnier. Inaugu-rated in 1880, it was designed to mirror Notre-Dame de Paris. Mass is held daily at 5.30am and 5pm, with seven Sunday ser-vices. Other visiting times are restricted (Mon–Sat 8–10.30am and 3–4pm).

The building to the right is the **General Post Office ⑤** (daily 7am–8pm), another impressive colonial-era edifice and one which has been re-painted of late follow-ing a broadly unpopular change of hues.

NGUYEN HUE AND HAM NHE STREETS

Head back to Lam Son Square and look to the northern end of Nguyen Hue Street for the lavish **People's Commit-tee Building ⑥** (UBND Thanh Pho). Formerly the French administrative headquarters, this is one of the city's loveliest landmarks. An imposing statue of Ho Chi Minh stands in front.

Turn into **Nguyen Hue Street**, formerly Boulevard Charner and today an eclec-tic jumble of old and new architecture, as well as the city's first fully pedestrian walkway. Note the old bank building at

The nightlife scene   *The People's Committee Building*

No. 37 on your right as you head towards the river. The facade, in charming colonial style, has been retained, while modern high-rises tower behind.

Turn right into Hai Trieu and continue until you reach the former **American Legation** ❼, on the corner of Ham Nghi and Ho Tung Mau streets. This striking 1950s block was where the character Pyle conducted his nefarious affairs close to Mr Muoi's bomb factory. On the other side of Ho Tung Mau is the new **Bitexco Financial Tower**. At 68 storeys, it is one of the tallest buildings in Vietnam, complete with its own on-functioning helicopter pad. It has recently opened an elevator ride to the top of the building, where tourists can get a 360-degree panorama of the city and take photos to their heart's content. The views are spectacular on a sunny day and the EON 51 bar is a great place to get a sundowner later in the day

Further up on the right, **Ton That Dam Street** was originally the location of 'Thieves' Market', where all manner of second-hand goods used to end up. Now this neighbourhood is a centre for Saigon's trade in pirated DVDs, digital music and electronics.

Round the day off with a cocktail at EON 51 (in the Bitexco) or the rather dated but well located **Rex Rooftop Garden Bar**, see ❷, at the Rex Hotel, overlooking The People's Committee Building. Then sample authentic, inexpensive Vietnamese street food at **Quan An Ngon**, see ❸, on Nam Ky Khoi Nghia Street, just two blocks south down Le Loi.

Food and drink

❶ L'USINE
151/1 Dong Khoi St; tel: 08 3521 0702; daily B, L & D; $$
Housed in a former garment factory, L'usine is a sleek modern cafe and lifestyle store serving excellent baguettes and light lunches, great coffee and a range of refreshing juices and shakes. A popular hangout for the Saigon hipster set.

❷ REX ROOFTOP GARDEN BAR
Rex Hotel, 141 Nguyen Hue Street; tel: 08-3829 2185; daily D; $$$
The fifth-floor open terrace offers bird's-eye views of downtown, and its giant crown, illuminated at night, is one of the city's best-known landmarks. The historic bar is a favourite of expats and visitors alike.

❸ QUAN AN NGON
138 Nam Ky Khoi Nghia Street; tel: 08-3825 7179; daily D; $$
Quang An Ngon is popular with both Vietnamese, tourists and expats thanks to its wide range of dishes from all over the country. From individual street kitchen style stalls a smorgasbord of Vietnamese seafood and popular cuisine is dished up in a lively atmosphere. Booking ahead is advised unless you are happy to queue for a table.

Reunification Palace

HO CHI MINH CITY: WAR REMNANTS

This one-day walking route takes you through Old Saigon's downtown District 1 and gives a glimpse into the former capital's wartime past through museums, shopping for war memorabilia and an atmospheric stroll.

DISTANCE: A 4km (2.5-mile) walk
TIME: A full day
START: Reunification Palace
END: Antique Shops at Le Cong Kieu Street
POINTS TO NOTE: This is a relatively comfortable walking tour through downtown Ho Chi Minh City. It can be intermingled with route 1 too. Be mindful of valuables while walking on the street, as snatch-and-run thievery is on the increase in this area.

On 30 April 1975, the camera that had focused on South Vietnam for decades was abruptly blanked out. The final images seen in the West were those of the fall of the South Vietnamese capital, Saigon: the roof of the US Embassy where the last departing helicopter was battling with crowds scrambling for space, and tanks storming through the Presidential Palace. What followed were 15 years of deprivation and austerity as the victorious Northerners imposed their land reform and free trade restrictions on the Southerners.

Since the 1990s, however, Ho Chi Minh City (Thanh Pho Ho Chi Minh) has risen, phoenix-like, from the ashes of former Saigon. This sprawling mass of humanity is Vietnam's commercial and economic hub, and the nation's largest and most populated city.

REUNIFICATION PALACE

Take a taxi or walk to the **Reunification Palace ❶** (Hoi Truong Thong Nhat; tel: 08-3822 3652; daily 7.30–11am, 1–4pm; charge) at the junction of Nam Ky Khoi Nghia Street and Le Duan Boulevard. It was formerly known as the Presidential Palace and headquarters of the Government of South Vietnam; work on the edifice started shortly before President Diem's assassination in 1963. The architect, Ngo Viet Thu, a 1960s purist, designed details from chandeliers to carpets specifically for the palace, making it one of the few totally contemporary state buildings of this era.

Inside the entrance are poster-size photographs of the 1970s. One of these is the famous image taken by NBC's Neil

Davies of a Russian tank forcing down the palace gates on 30 April 1975, spelling the demise of South Vietnam and its government. General Duong Van Minh, South Vietnam's president for just 24 hours, surrendered to the Northern forces minutes later.

The optional guided tour takes in several floors, including the cabinet meeting room, president's private residential quarters and cinema, plus bomb-proof basement, containing Nguyen Van Thieu's (president 1967–75) war operations rooms, complete with original war maps.

WAR REMNANTS MUSEUM

Walk north up Nam Ky Khoi Nghia Street to Vo Van Tan Street and turn left to find at No. 28 the **War Remnants Museum ❷** (Bao Tang Chung Tich Chien Tranh; 28 Vo Van Tan Street; tel: 08-3930 2112; daily 7.30am–noon, 1.30–5pm; charge), set in the former headquarters of the US Information Services. You need a strong stomach as the museum comes to grips with the nastier aspects of Vietnam's recent history, such as human embryos in jars and pictures of deformed children, depicting the effectiveness of the defoliant Agent Orange, gory photographs of war mutilations and a guillotine used for decapitating agitators in the 1920s riots. One of the exhibition halls, entitled **Requiem**, holds works of photographers from many

The Fine Arts Museum

Food and drink

① AU PARC
23 Han Thuyen Street; tel: 08-3829 2772;
daily B, L & D; $$$
Deco tile floors and high ceilings give
Au Parc a distinctly French ambience. A
choice of excellent baguette sandwiches,
in addition to a variety of Mediterranean
plates and *mezze*, are available indoors
on one of several air-conditioned floors
or outside on the patio, overlooking Le
Duan Park.

② SAIGON SAIGON BAR
Caravelle Hotel, 19 Lam Son Square; tel:
08-3823 4999; daily L & D; $$$
This rooftop bar not only boasts one
of the best downtown views from the
10th-floor, but during the Vietnam War it
was home to numerous American press
corps and became an infamous 'centre of
operations' for many war correspondents.
Stop here for a cocktail and to soak up
the city vistas.

③ SORAE SUSHI SAKE LOUNGE
76A (AB Tower), Le Lai; tel: 0838 272 372;
www.soraesushi.com; daily L & D; $$$$
Bringing upmarket Tokyo dining and
drinking to downtown Saigon, this is an
uber-chic venue with excellent Japanese
food, the longest sake menu in the land
and an extensive whisky and cocktail
selection to boot. Great views and sky-high
prices to go with them.

countries who died in war conflicts in
Indochina. Outside in the forecourt, there
is an impressive array of military hard-
ware, including tanks, a helicopter and a
fighter jet. Although a visit here is likely to
be distressing, it is a sobering reminder
of the heavy toll of war.

LE DUAN BOULEVARD AND CONSULATES

Backtrack towards the Reunification Palace. The gardens bordering the Palace
and Le Duan Boulevard were once the
palace gardens; now known as **Le Duan
Park ③**, this small oasis is edged by
cafés. Le Duan was previously Norodom
Boulevard, which developed as a diplomatic and residential enclave with pas-
tel-hued colonial villas. A fine example
still standing is the **French Consulate
General**, at No. 6, the only Western dele-
gation to remain open throughout 1975
and afterwards. Heading eastwards
along Le Duan, the next building on your
left is the **US Consulate General ④**,
constructed over the original embassy
building. In 1968, millions of television
viewers watched agape as a Viet Cong
special forces broke into the embassy
grounds during the Tet Offensive. The
original building had another, greater,
starring role when the last US helicopter
left from its grounds in 1975, carrying a
man aloft on a rope just seconds after
the US Ambassador swept his country's flag away in ignominy and stepped
into the helicopter. The new US Consu-

Portrait of Uncle Ho   *Stall at Dan Sinh Market*

late General, built after the half-derelict embassy was demolished in 1999, signifies a new era in US-Vietnamese relations. Diagonally across the road at No. 25 is the former British Embassy, now the **British Consulate General**.

At the eastern end of Le Duan, at No. 2, the **Ho Chi Minh Campaign Museum** ❺ (Bao Tang Chien Dich Ho Chi Minh; tel: 08-3822 9387; Sun, Tue–Fri 8–11.30am and Sun, Tue–Thur 1.30–4.30pm; charge) is devoted to recording the campaign by North Vietnamese communist troops as they captured the south in 1974–5.

For lunch, head back to Le Duan Park for lunch at **Au Parc**, see ❶.

WAR MEMORABILIA-SHOPPING

After lunch, take a taxi to **Dan Sinh Market** ❻ (Cho Dan Sinh), on the corner of Yersin and Nguyen Cong Tru streets. Also known as 'Yersin Market' or the 'War Surplus Market', it is slowly being dismantled, but stalls still sell a vast jumble of armed forces clothing, goods and wartime memorabilia. While a little stock is genuine vintage, most is new surplus or mass-produced reproduction.

Two blocks northeast, opposite the Fine Arts Museum, **Le Cong Kieu Street** ❼ has long been known as 'Antique Street'. Along this atmospheric small stretch, the row of narrow, open-fronted dwellings are devoted to sales of oriental and colonial bric-a-brac, furniture and decor, either reproduction or vintage.

Heading north, turn left on Nam Khi Koi Nghia Street and then take a right on Le Loi Street. **Caravelle Hotel**, at Lam Son Square (in front of the Municipal Theatre) has a perfect place for a pre-dinner cocktail at its **Saigon Saigon Bar**, see ❷. Follow up with dinner a short taxi ride west at the excellent **Sorae Sushi Sake Lounge**, see ❸.

Cu Chi Tunnels

Located about 70km (44 miles) to the northwest of HCMC, the Cu Chi Tunnels are one of Vietnam's proudest patriotic shrines and achievements during the Vietnam War. From these hiding places, Viet Cong were able to spring devastating surprise attacks. In fact, by the mid-1960s, it is believed that over 200km (124 miles) of tunnels laced the region around Cu Chi. The tunnels ran up to 10m (33ft) deep, each with a breadth of between 0.5 to 1m (1.5 to 3ft), and stacked up to three levels. The top tier could support the weight of a 50-tonne tank, while the middle layer could withstand moderate mortar attacks. The lowest level was virtually impregnable. Located at the end of the Ho Chi Minh Trail, and straddling both Highway 1 and the Saigon River, the tunnels were of vital strategic importance. However, some of the government's claims about the comfort and technological advances of the tunnels are unlikely.

Van Thanh Mieu temple in Vinh Long

THE MEKONG DELTA

This three-day trip to Vinh Long and Can Tho, in the heart of the Mekong Delta, lets you peek into the romantic ambience of the region. Meander through small waterways to floating markets and island gardens, and relax in munificent fruit orchards.

DISTANCE: Day 1: 140km (87 miles); Day 2: 246km (153 miles)
TIME: 3 days
START/END: Ho Chi Minh City
POINTS TO NOTE: Hire a car or motorcycle from the backpacker area in Ho Chi Minh City around De Tham and Pham Ngu Lao streets. Alternatively, a country bus ticket can be purchased at the bus station at the northern terminus of Pham Ngu Lao Street, in front of Ben Thanh Market. Plan to leave Ho Chi Minh City in the afternoon for the 138km (86-mile), three-hour journey, so that you arrive in Vinh Long in time to catch the sunset. For accommodation choices, see the Directory, page 102. There are many viable options for routes between HCMC and the cities in this tour, so be sure to bring a map. This tour is suitable for the whole family and is more about soaking up the landscape and ambience than visiting landmarks.

The Mekong River flows over 4,500km (2,800 miles) from the frozen wastes of Tibet through China, Laos, Cambodia and finally Vietnam before emptying into the sea. The nine provinces of the Delta area, beginning at Tan An, 40km (25 miles) from HCMC, are known as Cuu Long, or Nine Dragons, in reference to the nine tributaries of the Mekong. The number 9 is considered lucky in Vietnamese geomancy, and the Mekong Delta has certainly been lucky for its inhabitants. Silt from the Himalayan Plateau has made this area Vietnam's rice bowl. The delta is prone to extensive flooding, sometimes with serious consequences. During the rainy season months of May to November, some roads are impassable.

The Mekong Delta once belonged exclusively to the Khmers. The ancient archaeological site of Oc Eo, located in An Giang Province, was an important port city of the pre-Angkorian Funan Empire. Vietnam, however, downplays this history due to ethnic and political tensions.

Besides the Khmers and Chinese (or Hoa), the Cham are the other com-

Cai Rang floating market near Can Tho

mon minority in the Mekong. Cham Bani practise an ancient form of Islam blended with indigenous traditions of their cousins, the Cham Balamon of Binh Thuan and Ninh Thuan Province. Cham Islam is more recent, with influence from communities in Malaysia, Indonesia and the Middle East.

VINH LONG

Vinh Long ❶ is 34km (21 miles) from the municipality of Can Tho, the region's economic centre, and 70km (43 miles) from industrial My Tho. This provincial capital (the province is also named Vinh Long) sprawls along the southern shore of the Tien Giang, or Upper Mekong River. Although a city, Vinh Long is typical of this region: small, friendly and without a bustling centre. There are a few architectural remnants from French colonial times, a market and a handful of hotels, but,

as with this entire region, the main action is on and around the river.

In Vinh Long, secure a boat, either for the next day or to take you to your guesthouse on Binh Hoa Phuoc Island, if you have booked a homestay. For the latter, contact **Cuu Long Tourist** (tel: 070-382 3616; www.cuulongtourist. com), located on the ground floor of Cuu Long B Hotel at Number 1, 1 Thang 5 Street. Boats from Cuu Long Tourist are fairly expensive, but its English-speaking guides are well informed and can explain some of the area's mysteries to you. Alternatively, go to the An Binh Boat Station and negotiate.

Then settle back and enjoy the sunset over the Tien Giang River from the **Phuong Thuy Restaurant**, see ❶, located just across from the Cuu Long B Hotel.

Cai Be Floating Market

The next morning, meet your boatman for the three-hour return ride to **Cai Be Floating Market ❷** (daily 5am–5pm). This is a good place to eat breakfast or to buy a picnic lunch. Fresh produce, hand-woven baskets, palm sugar, buffalo horn and coconut utensils and a myriad of other goods are all on offer.

As you leave the dock, you will see people all along the riv-

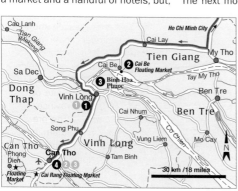

Trader at Cai Rang market

erbank tending to their household chores or washing (women bathe with all their clothes on) and children playing in the water. Many families have small sampans. Look out for the ones with great eyes painted red and black on their prows: these are ocean-going vessels, painted so they can see their way safely to the sea. You will see rice barges filled with seasonal, tropical fruits such as bananas, mangosteens and Java apples. Rice, fish and flowers are also traded from boats at the floating market. Along the shoreline, fish traps spear the water.

Binh Toa Phuoc Island

Head for **Nguyen Thanh Giao's (Ong Giao) House** in **Binh Hoa Phuoc ❸**, east of Vinh Long. The garden, filled with numerous bonsai trees, is an idyllic spot for a rest in a hammock with a book, and it is even better for lunch.

Study your map for other gardens and orchards to visit on An Binh and Binh Hoa Phuoc islands (or ask the boatman to recommend some). This is where a guide will help if you are interested in seeing how tropical fruits are grown. Rambutans, longans – the most important fruit in this area – mangoes and pineapples all produce abundant crops in the Mekong Delta's rich soil.

Elephant ear fish *(ca tai tuong)*, the local speciality, is as large as a soup plate and delicately flavoured. Sample some while you are on the island, wrapped in rice paper with salad, then dipped in a sauce.

CAN THO

In the evening travel 45 minutes' drive and 34km (21 miles) southwest of Vinh Long to the major ferry centre of **Can Tho ❹**, the largest town

Bridges and ferries

After a 2.5-hour drive from HCMC, you'll reach a suspension bridge just before Vinh Long. Previously the water was dotted with ferries. These huge clanking rafts carried everything from the school bus to street vendors and weather-beaten farmers. Only Ben Tre Province, Chau Doc City and a few minor roads are served by these lumbering machines today. The crossings are only a few minutes and will throw anyone enraptured by the French film *The Lover* into a romantic reverie.

Ferries have always been an essential part of life in the Mekong, which is prone to seasonal flooding. Some roads and many villages are inaccessible by road in the rainy season. They range from large wooden canoes with motors, which may carry people, livestock, merchant goods and motorbikes or farm equipment, to massive barges transporting cars, buses and trucks.

Exhibit at Can Tho Museum   *Making incense*

and effective capital of the Mekong Delta. Here the presence of Vietnam's substantial Khmer Krom community begins to make itself felt. **Munirangs-yaram Pagoda** at 36 Hoa Binh Street, for example, is a Therevada Buddhist temple very similar to those in Cambodia; minus the Bodhisattvas and Taoist spirits found in Vietnamese Mahayana temples.

Can Tho is a good place to stay overnight, as the accommodation available is the best in the delta, and good restaurants are aplenty. For food, head to **Nam Bo**, see ②, at 50 Hai Ba Trung along the waterfront, for seafood in comfortable surrounds.

Floating markets

It's a good idea to rise early and take a boat trip to see one of the local floating markets; but note that business slows down by 8.30am. There are two worthwhile floating markets near Can Tho: **Cai Rang** is about 5km (3 miles) southeast of the city centre, while **Phong Dien** lies about 20km (12 miles) to the southwest. If you're feeling energetic, Phong Dien is the better bet as it is less crowded.

After your watery shopping adventure, return to Can Tho for a leisurely lunch at **Spices**, see ③, in the Victoria Can Tho Hotel, and enjoy the river views. Don't stay too late, as it takes around three hours to drive back to Ho Chi Minh City.

Food and drink

① PHUONG THUY RESTAURANT

1, 1 Thang 5; tel: 070-382 4786; daily B, L & D; $$$

Phuong Thuy is a traditional Vietnamese restaurant offering great views of the Tien Giang River. The staff are friendly and helpful, even if their English isn't spot-on. Happily, it has an English-language menu and offers favourites like spring rolls (cha gio), fresh seafood, stir-fried noodles, fried rice, and caramelised pork in a clay pot.

② NAM BO

50 Hai Ba Trung; tel: 0710-382 3908; daily B, L & D; $$$

Nam Bo is set in a lovely French colonial villa along the waterfront and surrounded by gardens. Seating is indoors or on the upstairs terrace. The menu includes traditional Vietnamese and seafood as well as Western standards like pizza, soups, salads, sandwiches and pasta.

③ SPICES

Victoria Can Tho Hotel, Cai Khe Ward; tel: 0710-381 0111; daily B, L & D; $$$$

Seating at the featured restaurant of the Victoria Hotel is indoors or outside on the riverside terrace. The menu includes traditional Vietnamese and seafood, fine French, Italian and an American-style buffet. The restaurant is elegantly decorated in a Mekong theme, and service is excellent.

Poshanu Cham tower near Mui Ne

MUI NE AND AROUND

Frolic in Mui Ne, Vietnam's most popular beach resort, before taking an epic journey through desert landscapes, exploring some of the oldest monuments of the Champa Kingdom, in the modern homeland of the Cham people.

DISTANCE: Day 1: 150km (93 miles); Day 2: 50km (31 miles)
TIME: 2 days
START: Thap Po Shanu (Cham Temple in Phan Thiet)
END: Thap Po Klong Garai (Cham Temple in Phan Rang)
POINTS TO NOTE: This route is best used as a bridge between Ho Chi Minh City and Nha Trang. Phan Thiet, the gateway to Mui Ne, is accessible from HCMC by train and bus. Travel on this route is best by car or motorbike with a knowledgeable guide.

The ancient Champa Kingdom was a Hinduised, matriarchal culture, which at its height occupied all of central Vietnam and large sections of present-day Laos and Cambodia. Had a few wars turned out differently, Champa might have become Indochina's fourth country. Champa was eventually reduced to its southernmost province of Panduranga (modern Binh Thuan and Ninh Thuan prov-

inces). While there was later a mass exodus of Cham to Cambodia, and the kingdom was eventually dissolved by the Vietnamese King Minh Mang in 1832, the remaining Cham retain a thriving culture today.

Champa's architectural treasures are evident in their ancient red-brick temples scattered along the coast of Vietnam. In Panduranga alone there were dozens of such temples. Most here are mere vestiges, unmarked and lacking protection from any organised conservation effort.

PHAN THIET

The city of **Phan Thiet** is the capital of Binh Thuan Province. Its original Cham name was 'Hamu Lithit'. Today, it is best known for the beach at Mui Ne and as the home of perhaps Vietnam's best *nuoc mam* (fish sauce), and the centre of dragon fruit production.

While tourism and its associated activities in Mui Ne are an important engine of growth in Phan Thiet's economy, these two pillars of local com-

Strolling along Mui Ne Beach

merce existed long before the first pleasure-seeking tourists appeared, and have an even greater significance to the country as a whole. Dragon fruit comes from an enormous creeping cactus, native to Central and South America, where it is known as *pitaya*. With a preference for dry climates, it grows extraordinarily well in Binh Thuan and Ninh Thuan provinces, where it is known as *thanh long*, and produces some of the highest yields of the fruit in the world. Fish sauce, known in Vietnam as *nuoc mam*, is the foundation of Vietnamese cuisine. It's used as a seasoning, salt substitute, the base for broths and soups, and also a condiment. The best variety comes from Phan Thiet and Phu Quoc

island. *Nuoc cham*, a mix of fish sauce, water, lime juice, sugar, chilli and garlic, is the most common dipping sauce in Vietnam.

Thap Po Shanu

Begin at 8am at **Thap Po Shanu** ❶ (Km5 Nguyen Thong; 8am–5pm; charge) on a hilltop overlooking Phan Thiet, just west of Mui Ne. Here three temple towers now stand, and vestiges of several other structures, all built in the eighth century. This temple site is the southernmost in Vietnam, and one of the oldest standing Cham temples yet identified. According to scholars, it was originally devoted to Shiva, as indicated by the pair of phallic stone *linga-yoni* in the main tower.

A reclining Buddha near Phan Thiet

Po Shanu overlooks the **Phu Hai River**, which changes names to Cai and Song Quao as it flows upstream to the highlands. Cham lords established their quasi-independent territories along important river systems like this one, all along the coast of Vietnam. The Cham built temples along the rivers as their civilisations developed further upstream. Government archaeologists have located two others along this river system alone. There are probably many more.

Mui Ne

Drive east along **Mui Ne Beach** ❷, the resort and water-sports capital of Vietnam. This area (the real name of the area is Ham Tien; technically Mui Ne is just the name of the village on the cape at the end) first saw tourism when meteorologists designated it the best site in Vietnam to see the solar eclipse in 1995. This caught the attention of developers looking for fresh territory to stake out. Now tourists – many of them Russian – are coming to swim, sunbathe, enjoy the wealth of bars and restaurants and go kite-boarding, hugely popular here due to the regular high winds (Mui Ne has an average of 229 days a year with winds above 12 knots).

You'll pass a myriad of dining choices along the strip, the best of which include **Forest Restaurant**, **Joe's Café** and **Jibe's Beach Club** (all on the left side), see ❶, ❷ and ❸. Get breakfast along the beach and consider getting take-away sandwiches from Joe's, as you'll be limited to sparse options of Vietnamese street food the rest of the way.

White Sand Dunes

Drive north from Mui Ne Beach for 33km (20 miles) along the coast. On the way to the dunes, it's hard to miss the **titanium mining** operations along the highway. Some of the world's richest deposits are located in these dunes. Eventually you'll come to a beautiful lake system backed by immense dunes. Take the right fork along the lake and stop at the park entrance.

The **White Sand Dunes** ❸ are an immense Saharan range of undulating golden and snow-white dunes. Nestled at their base are two large reservoirs and a series of smaller lakes, which offer excellent opportunities to watch local birdlife. A number of small horses wonder the shores, enhancing the ambience. There are also village kids standing by, waiting to rent sleds to visitors for 'dune surfing'.

After a bit of fun, drive back west along the lake shore. Between the two lakes sits a **new shrine** under the trees. Here once stood an ancient Cham temple. Now the local Vietnamese residents worship the Cham goddess Po Nagar by another name: Tien Y A-Na. Continue driving north 14.5km (9 miles) to meet Highway 1.

White Sand Dunes

SONG LUY CITADEL

Turn left (west) on Highway 1 and drive for 5km (3 miles), watching closely for signs designating that you are in Song Luy. Take the first right on the dirt road going north to enter Song Luy proper. As you approach you will see orange citadel walls weaving between the houses.

According to extensive research by Adam Bray, **Song Luy ❹** (meaning 'River Fortification') is the site of **Ban Canan** (Bal Canar), the ancient imperial capital of Panduranga and last capital city of the Champa Empire. Ban Canan may have existed as Panduranga's capital for the better part of a millennium, but Po (King) Chai Paran moved Champa's imperial capital from Virapura (modern Phan Rang) to Ban Canan in 1653, at a time when the kingdom was waning thanks to Vietnamese southward expansion. The area was a key battleground during the Tay Son Rebellion of the late 1700s, which may account for why the citadel 'shows greater knowledge in the art of fortification than any other' in Vietnam. Although the victor of the rebellion, King Gia Long, awarded control of the area to the loyal Cham royal family, in 1822 his descendant, the emperor Minh Mang, dissolved all vestiges of Cham autonomy and Ban Canan fell into obscurity.

The citadel was built on the south banks of the **Luy River**, with earthen walls 7 to 10m (23 to 32ft) tall. Today they stand 1 to 6m (3 to 20ft). The total circumference is about 4km (2.5 miles). Walk around the city and climb the ramparts for views of the town and countryside. Residents of this city are, interestingly, not Cham but ethnic Nung and Hoa, strategically relocated from the far north by the government. The homes of the Nung are wooden, unlike those of their Vietnamese neighbours, with tiny balconies. Flags hang in their doorways with Chinese characters emblazoned. Be sure to stroll through the market at the centre of the village and try some of the unique northern cuisine, like *bun rieu cua* (rice noodle soup with crab meatballs).

THAP PO KLONG M'HNAI

From Song Luy, backtrack and drive east on Highway 1 for 4km (6 miles). You'll pass through the town of Luong Son. As the road veers left, on a hilltop to your right overlooking the river you will see the 17th-century **Thap Po Klong M'hnai ❺**, a temple complex dedicated to one of the last kings of Champa, along with his Cham wife and Vietnamese concubine. Three shrines stand here now, though originally there were five structures. Climb up the hill and have a look, but be aware that the complex is usually locked, so you'll have to view from outside the gate. If you happen to find yourself on the other side of the short fence, take a peek at the statues of the royal family, each inside their temple shrines.

Po Rome temple–tower

THAP PO DAM

It's another 22km to the town of **Phan Ri**. Phan Ri was one of the most important ports in Panduranga, known as 'Pa-Rik'. Many Cham kings, queens and court officials are buried in a veritable 'valley of the kings' here, though the royal cemeteries are unmarked and have recently fallen victim to looting.

Another 19km (12 miles) brings you through the town of **Lien Huong**, where the road veers north towards the mountains and meets the sea. Drive 4km (2.5 miles) north, and just before passing between the low mountains, take an unmarked dirt road to the left, veering north. You will cross a bridge over a canal and then the train tracks. Clearly situated on the mountain slopes you will see a set of Cham temples.

Thap Po Dam ❼ (daylight hours; free) was built in the ninth century and as such is one of the oldest standing temple complexes in Vietnam. It was originally a group of six temples, but now only three are standing. Legend says that this temple was built as part of a temple construction contest between two kings. Strangely, it is the only Cham temple complex to face southwards rather than towards the east.

Be careful not to disturb the rare Bray's Champa geckos (*Gekko champai*, sp.nov) that nest in the ruins and lay their eggs on the temple walls. These giant geckos were recently discovered and are endemic to this valley.

PHAN RANG

Back on the highway, it's another 50km (31 miles) north to the city of **Phan Rang** ❽. The twin cities of Phan Rang and Thap Cham comprise the provincial capital of Ninh Thuan Province, and are the focal point of the modern Cham homeland. The local economy is based on fishing, rice farming and, increasingly, tourism.

Check into your hotel in Phan Rang and get something to eat. Phan Rang lacks a good selection of restaurants catering to foreign visitors. The best option is to sample street food either at the **roundabout** at the intersection of Le Loi and Ngo Gia Tu streets, or the food stalls around the **central market** on Thong Nhat Street. Both locations are prominent landmarks. The roundabout is strictly outdoor seating, while the market has indoor and outdoor stalls. Local specialities include banh xeo (seafood pancakes), *sup cua* (crab soup) and *banh cuon* (fresh spring rolls).

Thap Po Rome and My Nghiep

Rise early in the morning, taking breakfast at the Central Market, and drive south on Highway 1, to the town of Phuoc Dan. At the intersection with road 703, take a brief detour, turning left to visit the craft village of **My Nghiep** ❾. Here you can observe traditional Cham weaving and purchase beautiful blankets and clothing. Afterwards backtrack and cross the highway, heading

King Po Rome as Shiva   *Workshop in Bau Truc*

north through Nhuan Duc village. About 15km (10 miles) south of Phan Rang on a hilltop sits the temple-tower of **Thap Po Rome** ⑩ (daylight hours; 'free' with tip for caretaker), named after a king of Champa who ruled from 1629 to 1651 and died a captive of the Vietnamese. The tower is one of the last built by the Cham, in the early 17th century. Four images of Po Rome sit in ascending enclaves on each side of the temple. Inside Po Rome is presented in the likeness of Shiva. A statue of his wife sits beside him.

Thap Po Klong Garai and Bau Truc

From Po Rome backtrack, heading north on road 703. Stop on the way at **Bau Truc** ⑪ craft village to see how Cham make traditional pottery without benefit of a kick wheel (and purchase a few pieces while you are there). Continue down the road and then turn west, driving another 7km (4 miles) towards Da Lat on Highway 27. You'll clearly see the three 14th-century towers, known as **Po Klong Garai** ⑫ (Thap Cham; daily 8am–6pm; charge) standing on an arid hill. The temple was built to worship King Po Klong Garai, who was acclaimed for constructing a much-needed local irrigation system. The entrance to the largest tower is graced with a dancing, six-armed Po Klong Garai represented as Shiva, and inside sits a statue of the bull Nandin.

After you've explored the temple, head back to Phan Rang for a late lunch.

Food and drink

① FOREST RESTAURANT (RUNG)

67 Nguyen Dinh Chieu Street; tel: 062-384 7589; www.forestrestaurant.com; daily L & D; $$$

The Forest Restaurant resembles a ruined Cham temple reclaimed by the jungle. Most of the staff are ethnic Cham, and live Cham music and dance shows go on all night. The menu includes traditional Vietnamese favourites and seafood.

② JOE'S CAFÉ

139 Nguyen Dinh Chieu Street; tel: 062-374 3447; daily B, L & D; $$

Joe's is the only local venue open 24 hours, offering Italian coffee, exceptional pizzas, burgers, pasta and a wide selection of sandwiches and breakfast dishes. The quality of food and service is very high. Live pop-rock music is performed nightly after 8pm.

③ JIBE'S BEACH CLUB

90 Nguyen Dien Chieu Street; tel: 06-23847008; www.windsurf-vietnam.com; daily B, L & D; $$

Popular with the kitesurfer crowd by day and a laid back dining spot by night, Jibe's is one of the most steadfastly popular places on the strip.

NHA TRANG

Beaches. Nightlife. Scuba diving. These four words encapsulate the Nha Trang experience for most travellers. For many Nha Trang is simply Vietnam's party town, yet the area is also home to museums and a rich ethnic culture.

DISTANCE: 7km (4 miles) by car
TIME: A full day
START: Po Nagar Cham Towers
END: Vinpearl Land Amusement Park
POINTS TO NOTE: Nha Trang is best reached from Mui Ne, Phan Rang or Da Lat by bus. From Danang, the train or a flight to nearby Cam Ranh is advised. Nha Trang is a family-friendly city with some of the best bars, restaurants and hotels outside HCMC and Hanoi. A hire car, motorbike or taxi will be necessary for this route.

Nha Trang is a place to break a journey, relax and soak up the sun, so long as you are happy on a beach backed by an increasing number of high rise hotels. The city has grown from a relatively backwater beach town to an internationally recognised holiday destination in just two decades. It is blessed with a beautiful **municipal beach** which fronts almost the entire city, along Tran Phu Street, a huge draw for Vietnamese tourists as well as thousands of Rus-

sians. There are always visitors basking in the warm sun and cool breezes at popular beach bars, and plenty of activities, whether jet skiing, sailing, windsurfing, parasailing or spending the day at an island amusement park.

PO NAGAR CHAM TEMPLE

Begin your tour where it all started: the ancient ruins of **Po Nagar** ❶ (2/4 Street, Vinh Hai Ward; tel: 058-383 1569; daily 6am–6pm; charge), on a hill above the **Cai River**. Only four of the sanctuary's original eight temples, all of which face east, remain standing. These were constructed over a long span of time between the seventh and 12th centuries. The 22 pillars and steep steps leading up to the main tower hint at the grandeur of the original temple.

The main tower is dedicated to the Cham goddess Po Yang Inu Nagar (worshipped by local Vietnamese as the goddess Thien Y A-Na), the 'Holy Mother' of the kingdom and considered by Cham to be a female manifestation of the Hindu god Shiva. Her statue resides in

Rainbow Divers hit the water

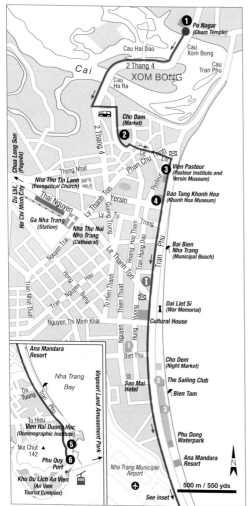

the main temple, but it was decapitated during French rule, and the original head is now in the Guimet Museum in Paris.

DAM MARKET

Some of Nha Trang's most interesting French colonial architecture and crumbling old Chinese taverns – as much as 200 years old – can be seen around **Dam Market ❷** near the Cai River. To get there, head south on Ha Ra Bridge via Street 2 Thang 4 and turn left. This former Chinese quarter is the most underrated part of town. The bustling market is surprisingly untouristed, and a welcome contrast to the rest of the modernised city, with its rustic and spontaneous atmosphere. It's a great place to snack while you explore: food is everywhere.

The Pasteur Institute

From Dam Market, head east to Tran Phu Street, where you will find the **Pasteur Institute ❸**

Alexandre Yersin Museum

(Vien Pasteur). The institute was founded in 1895 by Dr Alexandre Yersin, a French microbiologist, military doctor, explorer and overall Renaissance man (see box). Today the Institute still produces vaccines and carries out research, though with a very limited budget.

The small **Alexandre Yersin Museum** (10D Tran Phu; tel: 058-822 355; Mon–Fri 7.30–11am, 2–4.30pm; charge), displays many of Yersin's personal effects, furniture, documents and antique laboratory gadgets (including an enormous telescope). Many of his old books are kept in the library on display. This is the only portion of the institute open to the public.

KHANH HOA PROVINCIAL MUSEUM

Almost next door to the Pasteur Institute, the small **Khanh Hoa Museum** ❹ (Bao Tang Khonh Hoa; 16D Tran Phu Street; tel: 058-822 277; Tue–Fri 8am–11am, 2–5pm; free) can be explored thoroughly in about 15 minutes. The left wing contains relics from the Xom Con (*c.*3,000 years old), Dong Son (*c.*2000BC–AD200) and Champa (peak between seventh and 12th centuries) cultures. Notably absent are any of the otherwise ubiquitous exhibits about the previous wars or Uncle Ho found in most Vietnamese museums.

Afterwards, have lunch like a scuba diver, and consider (or at least dream about) signing up for some lessons at **Rainbow Divers**, see ❶. Get there by going south on Tran Phu, then turn right on Biet Thu, stopping at the corner of Hung Vong.

OCEANOGRAPHIC INSTITUTE

After lunch head south about 5km (3 miles) on Tran Phu Street, passing the Sailing Club, Louisiane and Bao Dai Villas (former holiday home of the last emperor). Sandwiched between the Bao Dai villas and Phu Quy Port, the **Oceanographic Institute** ❺ (1 Cau

Dr Alexandre Yersin

Alexandre Yersin arrived in Nha Trang in 1891 and was one of the first Europeans to extensively explore the Central Highlands and Mekong region south of Saigon. Yersin was also responsible for introducing Brazilian rubber trees and *quinquina* plantations – quinine-producing trees – to Vietnam at Suoi Dau, about 25km (15 miles) southwest of Nha Trang. He is buried here among his rubber trees, with a pagoda built nearby to worship him.

In 1894 Yersin was sent to Hong Kong by the French government and the Pasteur Institute to investigate an outbreak of bubonic plague. He soon discovered the link between rats, fleas, and eventually the bacterial cause. In 1895 he returned to Nha Trang and built a laboratory to manufacture the serum for the disease. In 1905 the lab became an official branch of the Pasteur Institute.

Da; tel: 058-590 036; daily 6am–6pm; charge) in Cau Da District was founded in 1923 and housed in a large French colonial complex. The institute has about a dozen large, open aquarium tanks. Most notable are the prowling sharks, inquisitive rays and seemingly oblivious sea turtles. A dozen smaller tanks are housed inside, showcasing bizarre reef fish and seahorses. The main building houses a massive collection of preserved specimens.

VINPEARL LAND AND AQUARIUM

Seen from Nha Trang's municipal beach, Hon Tre (Bamboo Island) is home to the **Vinpearl Land Amusement Park** (Hon Tre; tel: 058-958 188; www.vinpearl land.com; daily 8am–10pm; charge) and Vinpearl Resort. A gondola extending 3,320m (10,892ft) to the island departs from the **Phu Quy Port** , about 500m (1640ft) south of the Oceanographic Institute, and delivers visitors to the centre of the amusement park. The park contains a number of carnival rides and a roller coaster, games area, water park, outdoor shopping center and several restaurants.

The crowning feature of the park is the modern **Underwater World** with more than 20 freshwater and marine tanks of varying sizes, including a very impressive walk-through tank featuring sharks, rays, morays and a large variety of reef animals.

Afterwards, head back to the **Sailing Club** or **Louisiane Brewhouse**, see ❷ and ❸, for dinner and some nightlife.

Food and drink

❶ RAINBOW DIVERS

90A Hung Vuong; tel: 058-352 4351; www.divevietnam.com; daily B, L & D; $$$
The head office of Vietnam's top dive shop has an excellent bar and restaurant. The menu includes classic American, Australian and British grub.

❷ THE SAILING CLUB

72–74 Tran Phu; tel: 058-382 6528; www.sailingclubvietnam.com; daily B, L & D; $$$$
The Sailing Club is one of the best-known expat haunts in Vietnam. Directly on the beach and open late, it is an amalgamation of several unique eateries and bars, including the signature Sandals Restaurant. Menus include Indian, Italian, Western and Asian fusion.

❸ LOUISIANE BREWHOUSE

Lot 29, Tran Phu; tel: 058-352 1948; www.louisianebrewhouse.com.vn; daily B, L & D; $$$$
The Louisiane is the most chilled-out, yet opulent, beach hangout in town. The beachside restaurant with swimming pool offers mostly Vietnamese seafood, with some steaks, burgers, pizza and sushi thrown in. The microbrewery beers are a must-try.

Fresh produce and other goodies at Da Lat Central Market

DA LAT

An old colonial mountain resort, Da Lat was a favourite getaway for not only the French, but also the last emperor, Bao Dai. Escape the coastal heat, enjoy the abundance of fresh, local produce and stroll along Lake Xuan Huong below some of Vietnam's best colonial architecture.

DISTANCE: 10km (6 miles)
TIME: A full day
START: Da Lat Central Market
END: Da Lat Palace Golf Club
POINTS TO NOTE: Da Lat is the most walkable city in Vietnam. This tour is suitable for the entire family, and though the walk is up and down gentle hills, it is not challenging. This tour requires a mix of walking and rides in taxis or motorbikes. Da Lat also serves as the starting point for the Central Highlands road trip.

Da Lat is the capital of Lam Dong Province, resting at an elevation of 1500m (4921ft), on the Langbiang Plateau. The city is ideally situated as a vacation hub with major highways leading conveniently to HCMC, Phan Thiet, Phan Rang, Nha Trang and Buon Ma Thuat. With an average annual temperature of 17°C (63°F), Da Lat is Vietnam's most popular fair-weather retreat and one of the nation's top honeymoon destinations.

The original inhabitants of the area were the K'ho tribe, divided into the Lat and Chil clans. Da Lat literally means 'River of the Lat People', although much of the clan relocated to nearby Lat village as Da Lat grew. In addition to the K'ho, the Ma and Churu tribes also inhabit the hills surrounding Da Lat. Although largely forced to assimilate by the government, occasionally people can be seen walking about in quasi-traditional dress with large baskets hanging on their backs.

Dr Alexandre Yersin (see page 50) was the first European to survey the area in 1893, under the authority of Paul Doumer, the French governor-general of Indochina. Considered the founder of Da Lat, he recommended a hill station and sanatorium be built here to take advantage of the mild climate and beautiful scenery.

DA LAT CENTRAL MARKET

Begin at the **Da Lat Central Market** ❶. It is set in the deep hollow of a tall hillside and surrounded by rows of cafés

Central Market   *An abundance of flowers at the market*

and shops selling flowers, wine and candied fruit.

Food is the highlight here, with stalls selling rice meals with local specialities, and che, a desert made with sweetened beans and candied fruit. The stairs and ramps leading to the market are also flanked with vendors in the evening, selling grilled meats, corn, sweet potatoes, and rice crackers topped with quail-egg omelettes; *sua dau nanh* (hot, fresh soy milk); *banh cam* (sesame doughnuts filled with green-bean paste); sweet waffles stuffed with cheese and pork; and bowls of steamed snails. The takeaway specialities sold throughout the market include dried and candied fruits, wines and deer jerky. Grab some breakfast here.

The market is bustling well before 6am and remains open long past 11pm. On Saturdays and Sundays from 7–10pm, the streets surrounding the market are closed to vehicles and a carnival atmosphere ensues with an influx of pedestrians, souvenir peddlers, food vendors and street-side clothing auctioneers.

DA LAT CATHEDRAL

From the market, walk south on Le Dai Hanh (the lake will be on your left), then straight ahead is the tan- and cream-colored **Da Lat Cathedral** ❷

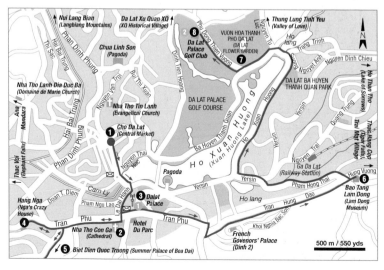

Bust of Emperor Bao Dai

(Nha Tho Con Ga or 'Rooster Church'; Mon–Sat Mass 5.15am and 5.15pm, Sun Mass 5.15am, 7am, 8.30am, 4pm and 6pm). The cathedral was built in 1942, with stained-glass windows made by Louis Balmet, in Grenoble, France. The rooster weather vane on top of the steeple lends the church its nickname.

DA LAT PALACE AND HOTEL DU PARC

Da Lat was originally built around the grand Langbian Palace Hotel, now known as the **Da Lat Palace ❸**. Construction of the hotel began in 1902 and finished 20 years later (at the time, travel from the coast took more than a week, making construction difficult). The **Hotel Du Parc** followed in 1932. Both retain much of their original architectural charm. Both hotels sit to the left of the cathedral, on either side of Tran Phu Street. **Le Café de la Poste**, see ❶, between the two hotels (and owned by the same company), makes a great breakfast or lunch stop.

NGA'S CRAZY HOUSE

Head west on Tran Phu Street now, then turn south (left) at the triangular roundabout onto 3 Thang 2 Street. Finally take a right on Huynh Thuc Khang. For anyone travelling with children, or those who played in treehouses themselves as a child, **Nga's Crazy House ❹** (Hang

Nga; 3 Huynh Thuc Khang; tel: 063-382 2070; daily 7am–6pm; charge) is a whimsical and inspiring architectural delight for the whole family. The never-ending house is continuously being added to, with tunnels, stairways and halls meandering into secret rooms, towers and reading nooks, occupied by giant carved kangaroos, giraffes, eagles and bears.

SUMMER PALACE OF BAO DAI

Walking less than a kilometre further south on 3 Thang 2 Street, and turning left on Trieu Viet Vuong Street, brings you to the **Summer Palace of Bao Dai ❺** (Biet Dien Quoc Truong; Duong Trieu Viet Vuong; tel: 063-382 6858; daily 7.30am–11am, 1.30–4pm; charge), Vietnam's last emperor, which was built between 1933 and 1938. This is the third of the palaces (designated Dinh I, Dinh II and Dinh III) belonging to Bao Dai in Da Lat, although the other two are not currently open to the public. It's said that all three are connected by tunnels so that the emperor could secretly visit his mistresses in each one.

LAM DONG MUSEUM

Grab a taxi or motorbike and head back to Tran Phu Street, which turns into Tran Hung Dao and then Hun Vuong. Da Lat's **Lam Dong Museum ❻** (Bao Tang Lam Dong; 04 Hung Vuong; tel: 063-382 2339; daily 7.30am–11.30am,

Lam Dong Museum

Nga's Crazy House

1.30–4.30pm; charge) is an excellent museum, recognised by the United Nations for its extensive collection of musical gongs, used by the local K'ho, Ma and Churu minorities. Exhibits also include a very impressive taxidermy collection of local wildlife; relics from the Funan Empire, excavated at Cat Tien National Park; artefacts found in recent excavations from yet-unidentified cultures; and full-sized Ma and K'ho longhouses, decorated with musical instruments, weapons and common household items.

XUAN HUONG LAKESIDE

Catch a taxi or motorbike to any stretch along **Xuan Huong Lake** to continue your walk. Formerly part of the town's colonial-era golf course before it was flooded, the lake sprawls through the heart of the town. The surrounding hills, villas and pine forests provide a lovely backdrop.

Da Lat Flower Garden
Walk to the north side of the lake and visit the **Da Lat Flower Garden** ❼ (2 Tran Nhan Tong; tel: 063-355 3545; 7am–6pm; charge). The best time to visit the gardens is during the annual **Da Lat Flower Festival**, usually held for a week in November, December or January (dates and activities vary from year to year), when there are beautiful flower displays in the gardens, surrounding a small lake.

Da Lat Palace Golf Club
On the northern banks, a golf course originally built for the last emperor, Bao Dai, has been renovated and expanded into the lovely **Da Lat Palace Golf Club** ❽. The 18-hole championship course is a sister location to the Ocean Dunes Golf Club in Phan Thiet. They also have a great restaurant to watch the sunset over the green, see ❷.

Food and drink

❶ LE CAFÉ DE LA POSTE
Tran Phu Street; tel: 063-382 5444; daily B, L & D; $$$$
This charming French-style café serves a select menu of sandwiches, pasta, Asian and French dishes. Service is friendly, and meals are prepared with great care. Even the toasted ham and cheese sandwich is a memorable treat. The buffet breakfast is excellent.

❷ DA LAT PALACE GOLF CLUB
Phu Dong Thien Vuong Street; tel: 063-382 1201; daily B, L & D; $$$$
Set in the original colonial club-house, the restaurant serves Tex-Mex, Korean, Japanese, Thai and Vietnamese specialities. The home-made chips and salsa, buffalo wings and chicken fingers are all top-notch. Outdoor seating offers a lovely view of the greens and lake while you eat.

Elephant Falls

CENTRAL HIGHLANDS

Spend a few days on the open road, exploring Vietnam's mountainous interior by car or motorbike. The region is populated by hill-tribe minorities in a landscape of tea and coffee plantations, peppered with waterfalls and elephant herds.

DISTANCE: 373km (232 miles)
TIME: 3 days
START: Da Lat
END: Buon Ma Thuot
POINTS TO NOTE: This route forms a continuation of route 6 and a possible bridge to route 5. This road trip can be taken by private car or motorbike, ideally with a guide. Da Lat's 'Easyriders', a loose association of motorbike guides, are a popular option. Just stand on the street above Da Lat's Central Market and one will find you. Usually no particular preparations are needed when you travel with a guide; they tend to take care of all your needs. The most popular tour company is Phat Tire Ventures, 73 Truong Cong Dinh; www.ptv-vietnam.com; tel: 063-382 9422.

Vietnam's Central Highlands include the provinces of Gia Nghia, Lam Dong, Dak Lak, Gia Lai and Kon Tum. The area has historically been home to many ethnic minorities, including the Ma, K'ho, Jarai, Ede and Bahnar. Many of them, particularly in the north, were subjects of the former Champa Kingdom, but gradually brought under the dominion of the French and eventually the Vietnamese.

The highlands are a major agricultural centre for Vietnam, where crops include coffee, tea, black pepper, vegetables, flowers and corn. Unlike coastal areas, relatively little rice is grown here. The cities of the Central Highlands are quite new. Most were built by the French and continued as American military bases during the war.

FROM DA LAT

Leave early in the morning (the earlier the better) from **Da Lat ❶**. The first day of driving 156km (97 miles) north on Highway 27 is mostly about enjoying the scenery through tea and coffee plantations, with quick stops for photos.

Elephant Falls
Elephant Falls ❷ (Thac Voi; free), 30km (19 miles) west of Da Lat, is a favourite stop for most countryside tours from

A cable-car ride near Da Lat offers panoramas of villages and mountain forests

Dalat. The dramatic rock formations are just as interesting as the falls themselves, which look like a movie set from Peter Jackson's *King Kong*. It's a bit of a climb down to the bottom of the falls, but natural-looking stairs have been skilfully built into the rocks to make the way easier. A shop above the falls sells beautiful hand-woven K'ho blankets and crafts, all made on-site.

On your way to Lak Lake, you will pass many different **farms** specialising in roses and other flowers, mushrooms, silk, black pepper, coffee and tea plantations, and even rice-wine distilleries. To visit these, it is essential to have a guide, as they are not signposted and do not have their own guides to provide tours.

LAK LAKE

The shores of **Lak Lake** are inhabited by displaced members of the M'nong tribe, relocated here from the north by the government. The M'nong number about 50,000 and are matriarchal. The M'nong have been famed elephant-catchers for hundreds of years, although their elephants are now used for tourist rides rather than dragging logs from the forest.

Night in a longhouse

Spend the night in one of the immense wooden

Ako Dhong village, near Buon Ma Thuot

M'nong longhouses on the lake (they are available for evening rentals at the tourism office in front of Buong Jun village). Be advised that sleeping is on a mat on the floor, under a mosquito net, and bathrooms are a communal outhouse.

Boat rides

Rise early the next morning and explore the lake by dugout. The canoes are painstakingly hollowed out from tree trunks by axe. Two people can sit in the boats, with a driver in the back. This is a good way to view the mountain scenery and watch the village kids riding their water buffalos as they swim across the lake.

Villages

A number of villages can be visited by boat. The best Ede village to visit is **Buon Tur**, while **Buon Jun** is inhabited by M'nong. Villagers live in tall longhouses. Families depart in a mass exodus early each morning to herd cattle, fish in the lake, or gather resources from the countryside, returning home at dinner time.

DRAY SAP, DRAY NUR AND GIA LONG WATERFALLS

After a quick lunch, drive north on Highway 27. At the 22km (13.5mile) marker, south of Buon Ma Thuot, take Road 690 west to Highway 14. Drive 8km (5 miles) south, then take the marked left turnoff 3km (2 miles) to the entrance of **Dray Sap, Dray Nur and Gia Long waterfalls** ④ (tel: 0500-385 0123; daily 7am–5pm; charge). There are toilets and a café at the entrance where a light lunch can be had. Sadly, there is also a rather sad-looking small zoo on the grounds

Originating from Cu Yang Sin Mountain, the three waterfalls of Dray Sap, Dray Nur and Gia Long form a 100m (328 ft) wide cascade. They are particularly stunning in the wet season, although Dray Sap and Dray Nur are impressive even in the dry season.

YUK DON NATIONAL PARK

Drive another hour north and spend the evening inside **Yok Don National Park** ⑤ (Vuon Quoc Gia Yok Don, Buon Don District; tel: 500-378 3049; email: yokdonecotourism@vnn.vn; charge). Limited dining is available at the park ranger station, or the food stalls in **Ban Don village**, just a couple of kilometres further up the road.

This 115,545-hectare (45,760-acre) wildlife reserve contains at least 63 species of mammals and 250 species of birds. More than 15 of these animals are listed as endangered. There are known to be Asian elephants (including rare white elephants), tigers, giant muntjac, Samba deer, golden jackal, leopard and green peafowl living in the park, but the chance of seeing any of these is almost zero.

Dray Sap waterfall   *Ducks at market in Buon Ma Thuot*

Rise early the next morning for an elephant and boat ride. Plan to leave the park by noon.

BUON MA THUOT

Drive two hours southeast and arrive at **Buon Ma Thuot** ⑥, the capital of Dak Lak Province, as well as the capital of Vietnam's coffee production. Have a late lunch at **Bon Trieu** at 33 Hai Ba Trung Street or Bui Saigon, see ① and ②.

Museum of Ethnology
After lunch, head just south of the city centre to the corner of Le Duan and Y Nong Streets. Dak Lak's **Museum of Ethnology** (Y Nong Street; Tue–Sun 7.30–11am, 2–5pm; charge) is an impressive piece of architecture modelled on a traditional long house and has one of the finest collections of Central Highlands hill-tribe crafts and relics, outside the Hanoi Museum of Ethnology. The collection includes intricate costumes, rice-wine jars, musical instruments and baskets of K'ho, Ede, Ma, Jarai, S'tieng and Bahnar.

Exploring the city
A few **Ede villages** lay on the outskirts of town, such as Ako Dhong, and are worth visiting if there is still daylight. Around Ly Thuong Kiet Street are some of the only **craft shops** in Vietnam where authentic crafts of Central Highlands hill tribes can be purchased. Have dinner at one of the *nem nuong* **restaurants** in the neighborhood, see ③.

Going further
From Buon Ma Thuot, you have a choice of continuing on to Pleiku (five hours to the north) and then Kon Tum (another two hours), or heading out to the coast north of Nha Trang (an all-day drive). All of the drives have beautiful scenery, and Kon Tum has fascinating Bahnar and Jarai villages.

Food and drink

① BON TRIEU
33 Hai Ba Trung, tel: 05-3851 2994
For those seeking a diversion from Vietnamese food, Bon Trieu offers some reasonable Western fare alongside some local classics.

② BUI SAIGON
11 Le Hong Phong; tel: 05-0385 6040
One of a few popular eateries on this small strip, Bui Saigon serves up grilled pork and chicken topped rice at bargain basement prices.

③ NEM NUONG RESTAURANTS
East side of Ly Thuong Kiet Street, between No Trang Long & Quang Truong streets; daily B, L & D; $
Nem nuong are roll-it-yourself fresh spring rolls with grilled meats, fresh herbs, pickled vegetables and boiled eggs. This strip of restaurants is conveniently located amidst the town's most popular budget accommodation.

HOI AN OLD TOWN

Hoi An retains its old-town atmosphere and architecture as a World Heritage Site, yet has become one of Vietnam's top tourism and shopping destinations, despite its diminutive size. Spend your days exploring old temples and ancient shop houses, and visiting the surrounding beaches and craft villages.

DISTANCE: 4km (2.5-mile) walk
TIME: One busy day or two leisurely days with lots of shopping and café breaks
START: Le Loi Street Ticket Office
END: Quan Thang House
POINTS TO NOTE: Hoi An is best reached by plane or train to nearby Da Nang. This route can be grouped with the Cham Holy Land tour. Hoi An is one of the most popular, family-friendly destinations in Vietnam. It is often quite busy with tourists, but rising very early is one good way to see it at its quietest; Hoi An Photo Tours run sunrise and sunset tours in less tourist-heavy areas (www.hoianphototour.com). Hoi An is also one of the few wheelchair-friendly towns in the country.

About 25km (15 miles) southeast of Da Nang, the ancient town of **Hoi An** nestles on the banks of the **Thu Bon River**. Originally a seaport in the Champa Kingdom, by the 15th century it had become a coastal Vietnamese town under the Tran Dynasty. At the beginning of the 16th century, the Portuguese came to explore the coast of Hoi An. Then came the Chinese, Japanese, Dutch, British and French.

Hoi An appeared in Western travelogues in the 17th and 18th centuries as Faifo or Hai Po. For several centuries Hoi An was one of the most important trading ports in Southeast Asia. By the beginning of the 19th century the mouth of the Thu Bon silted up and another port was built at the mouth of the Han River. Thenceforth Da Nang replaced Hoi An as the centre of trade.

In the early 1980s, Unesco and the Polish government funded a restoration programme to classify and safeguard Hoi An's old quarters and historic monuments. Hoi An was designated a Unesco World Heritage Site in 1999.

An admission ticket of VND120,000 (sold by various entry gate booths around the perimeter) gains you entry to five of the sites including four museums, four old houses, three assembly halls, the Handicraft Workshop (with traditional music concert), and the Japanese Bridge and the Quan Cong Temple. Most sites are open daily from 7am

Hoi An

to 6pm and require an Old Town Ticket, unless otherwise noted.

DAY 1: THE WEST SIDE AND JAPANESE QUARTER

Le Loi Street is centrally located and a good place to start your exploration. Heading south towards the river, buy your ticket at the **ticket office ①** on your right as you enter the Old Quarter.

Cantonese Assembly Hall and Sa Huynh Museum

Turn right on Tran Phu Street and head to the **Cantonese Assembly Hall ②** (Hoi Quan Quang Dong; 176 Tran Phu Street), founded in 1786. It's a pleasant spot with an amusing fountain in the middle of the courtyard, composed of a twisted dragon set to devour a carp, and a turtle spying from behind. It's all beautifully decorated in colored ceramic tiles. Large red coils of incense hang from the ceilings, hung by numerous families as offerings.

Across the street, the **Museum of Sa Huynh Culture ③** (Bao Tang Van Hoa; 149 Tran Phu Street; daily 8am–5pm) has a nice collection of ancient pottery and jewellery from local excavations.

Japanese Covered Bridge

One of the most remarkable architectural pieces in town is the **Japanese Covered Bridge ④** (Cau Nhat Ban/Lai Vien Kieu). Built by the Japanese community in the 16th century, it links the Chinese and Japanese quarters, and Tran Phu Street with Nguyen Thi Minh Khai. The bridge's curved

Map labels:

Life Heritage Resort
Hoi Quan Trieu Chau (Chaozhou Chinese Assembly Hall) **⑩**
Duy Hieu
Nguyen
Cau Cam Nam
Cam Nam
Hoang Dieu
Hai Nam Hoi Quan (Hainan Chinese Assembly Hall) **⑪**
Chua Quan Cong (Temple)
Thu Bon
Bao Tang Van Hoa va Lich Su Hoi An (Hoi An Museum of History & Culture)
Nguyen Hue
Cho Hoi An (Central Market) **⑨**
Hoi An Artcraft Manufacturing Workshop **⑧**
Hoi Quan Phuc Kien (Fujian Chinese Assembly Hall) **⑫**
Chua Ba (All-Chinese Assembly Hall)
Tran Hung Dao
Bao Tang Gom Su (Museum of Trading Ceramics)
Tran Phu
Nguyen
Museum of Folklore in Hoi An **⑦**
Nha Tho Ho Tran
Nha Co Quan Thang (Quan Thang House) **⑬**
Thai
Bach Dang
Da Nang
Le Loi
Le Loi
Phan Chu Trinh
Ticket Office **①**
Nha Tho Ho Truong
Hoc
Nha Co Tan Ky (Tan Ky House) **⑥**
Tran Phu
Hoi Quan Quang Dong (Cantonese Assembly Hall)
Nhi Trung
Ban Dao An Hoi
Bao Tang Van Hoa (Museum of Sa Huynh Culture) **③**
Phan Dinh Phung
Cau Nhat Ban/Lai Vien Kieu (Japanese Covered Bridge) **④**
Ba Trieu
Nha Co Phung Hung (Phung Hung House) **⑤**
My Son
200 m / 220 yds

Tan Ky House

shape and undulating green- and yellow-tiled roof give the impression of moving water. According to legend, a monster with his head in India, his tail in Japan and his heart in Hoi An was causing local calamities. The bridge was erected at the heart to kill this monster, known as 'Cu'. Tradition also states that the bridge was started in the year of the monkey and finished in the year of the dog. Thus, a stone pair of each now stands at either end of the bridge as guardians.

Phung Hung and Tan Ky Houses

The **Phung Hung House** ❺ (Nha Co Phung Hung; 4R Nguyen Thi Minh Khai Street; free), which has Japanese and Chinese architectural influences, is still family-owned after nearly 230 years. They give guided tours, a free tea service, have an embroidery shop in the back and a gift shop upstairs.

From here, turn back to the covered bridge and make your way to the right on Nguyen Thai Hoc Street, continuing until you reach the **Tan Ky House** ❻ (Nha Co Tan Ky; 101 Nguyen Thai Hoc Street; daily 8am–noon, 2–4.30pm). Typical of the old houses in Hoi An, it is a two-storey home built of finely decorated precious wood. An inner courtyard is open to the sky, with a veranda linking several living quarters. Although many of the old Hoi An homes have been restored over the years, they retain their original wooden framework, carved doors and windows, and sculpted stuccos, as well as very rare antiques from

Vietnam, China, Japan and France. Likewise, one of the most remarkable features of these old homes is their amalgamation of these cultures within the architecture itself.

For lunch or dinner, head to **Streets Restaurant Cafe**, a training restaurant for disadvantaged young people, see ❶, on Le Loi Street at the north edge of the Old Town.

DAY 2: THE EAST SIDE AND FRENCH QUARTER

Start from where the previous day's tour finished off and walk west on Nguyen Thai Hoc Street.

The Museum of Folklore, Handicraft Workshop and Central Market

The **Museum of Folklore in Hoi An** ❼ (33 Nguyen Thai Hoc Street; tel: 051-091 0948; daily 8am–5pm; free) is in an old house with a craft shop downstairs and an excellent museum upstairs, featuring exhibits of artisan tools, ancient crafts and local folklore.

The **Hoi An Artcraft Manufacturing Workshop** ❽ ('Handicraft Workshop', 9 Nguyen Thai Hoc Street) is located in a 200-year-old Chinese merchant shop. Lanterns and other souvenir crafts are made and sold in the back of the shop. The main draw is the traditional music and dance show at 10.15am and 3.15pm each day.

Continue east and make your way through the **Central Market** ❾ (Cho

Chaozhou Chinese Assembly

Inside Phung Hung House

Hoi An; free), a great place to pick up snacks and fresh fruit and to find better bargains than in most street shops.

Assembly Halls and Quan Thang House
Turn left on Hoang Dieu Street, heading northwest. Then turn right on Nguyen Duy Hieu, heading northeast to the **Chaozhou Chinese Assembly Hall** ⑩ (Hoi Quan Trieu Chau, opposite 157 Nguyen Duy Hieu Street; daily 8am–5pm), built in 1776. The altars are some of the finest examples of wood-carving motifs in Hoi An. The roofs of the structure are decorated with elaborate miniature figures of soldiers, deities, dragons and mythical beasts, all composed of colourful ceramic tiles.

Backtracking on Nguyen Duy Hieu, consider a refreshment stop at **Moon Restaurant**, see ②, before the street becomes Tran Phu. The **Hainan Chinese Assembly Hall** ⑪ (Hai Nam Hoi Quan; 10 Tran Phu Street; daily 8am–5pm; free) was built in 1851 and is a memorial to 107 Chinese merchants who were murdered by a rogue commanding officer in Emperor Tu Duc's navy. Ton That Thieu had looted the ships and claimed that pirates were responsible, but his crimes were later discovered and he was gruesomely executed along with his officers.

Continue on Tran Phu Street to the **Fujian Chinese Assembly Hall** ⑫ (Hoi Quan Phuc Kien; across from 35 Tran Phu Street). The largest and most elaborate of the assembly halls in town, it was turned into a temple to Thien Hau

and houses idols of numerous Chinese deities. Worshippers believe Thien Hau rescues sailors from sinking ships.

Finally, the **Quan Thang House** ⑬ (77 Tran Phu Street) is more than 300 years old and has been in the current family for six generations. It is sparsely decorated with two family altars and a small courtyard.

Food and drink

① STREETS RESTAURANT CAFÉ

17 Le Loi Street; tel: 05-103911948; www.streetsinternational.org; daily B, L & D; $$

A training restaurant for disadvantaged youth, Streets is not only a place to give back, but also to try some very well prepared Hoi An classics. The service is excellent and it's normally busy making for a good atmosphere. The sangria is recommended.

② MOON RESTAURANT & LOUNGE

321 Nguyen Duy Hieu; tel: 0510-324 1396; www.hoianmoonrestaurant.com; daily B, L & D; $$

Service is very friendly at this classical Vietnamese restaurant with a modern twist, set in an old French colonial building with wooden interiors and decorated with a gallery of paintings. It is certainly aimed at tourists, but this is a long-running outfit with good reason. It has a cosy atmosphere and a nice bar.

Museum of Cham Sculpture, Da Nang

CHAM HOLY LAND

Take a day or two's drive through some beautiful coastal scenery and Vietnam's third-largest city of Da Nang on your way to visiting the holiest sites and relics of the ancient Champa Kingdom.

DISTANCE: 93km (58 miles)
TIME: A long day by car, or two day trips
START: Museum of Cham Sculpture, Da Nang
END: The Cargo Club, Hoi An
POINTS TO NOTE: Da Nang is best reached by train from Hue, or by air from Cam Ranh near Nha Trang. This trip can be grouped with route 8 and is generally suitable for the whole family. My Son requires a lot of walking, and visitors must stay on marked paths. Landmines may still exist off the beaten path, so take care and stick to the beaten ones.

The Champa Kingdom once occupied the area of Da Nang, Hoi An and Quang Nam Province, known collectively as Amaravati, for a thousand years. While most of the Cham were pushed south to Binh Thuan and Ninh Thuan provinces (the Cham province of Panduranga), remnant tribes of the ancient multi-ethnic kingdom still live in the area. The Cham holy city of My Son and the

Da Nang Museum of Cham Sculpture together form one of the greatest collections of Champa art and architecture. The Marble Mountains, which once housed Cham shrines, makes for a pleasant interlude.

Have breakfast before you start or brunch after the museum, at the superb **Bread of Life**, see ❶, at the Bach Dang and Dong Da roundabout. Afterwards, drive south on Tran Phu Street until it terminates at the museum.

MUSEUM OF CHAM SCULPTURE

Begin your tour at Da Nang's **Museum of Cham Sculpture** ❶ (Bao Tang Dieu Khac Champa; Number 2, 2 Thang 9 Street; daily 8am–5pm; charge). This extensive collection of superbly preserved statuary was established in 1915 by the École Française d'Extrême-Orient (EFEO). Buy the useful booklet (*Museum of Cham Culture – Danang*) written by the museum curator, Tran Ky Phuong, on sale at the entrance.

You will walk through rooms featuring four different periods (displayed

Marble Mountains

somewhat haphazardly) dating from the seventh to the 15th century, according to their city of origin: My Son, Tra Kieu, Dong Duong and Thap Mam. The wealth of Hindu relics removed from My Son and neighbouring Tra Kieu represent some of the finest examples of Cham art. Dong Duong was a Buddhist enclave in the Champa Kingdom, also found in Quang Nam Province. Thap Mam, located far south in Quy Nhon, represents the decline of Champa, when the art had become rather stylised.

The museum contains the largest display of Cham artefacts in the world. At the centre of the museum you will see the deity Ganesh with his elephant head, recurring examples of Shiva dancing in his warlike manner, Nandin the bull mount of Shiva and many other figures, all sensuously erotic and finely carved.

The temples of Champa generally followed one basic, three-storey design. They represent Mount Meru, the Hindu abode of the gods, and generally face east towards the rising sun. The inner sanctum normally had a Shivalinga at its centre.

THE MARBLE MOUNTAINS

Take any of the bridges east across the Han River, then drive south on either coastal road to the **Marble Mountains** ❷ (Ngu Hanh Son). Each is named for one of the five Daoist phases of Wu Xing: Kim Son (metal), Thuy Son (water), Moc Son (wood), Hoa Son (fire) and Tho Son (earth). Caves within the mountains were once used by Cham and now shelter altars dedicated to Buddha, various bodhisattvas and the local deities worshipped by the area's inhabitants.

Huyen Kong Cave

Ancient Champa

The Kingdom of Champa may have been established around the second century, and for about 1,000 years (5th–15th century) it flourished in this region of Vietnam. At its apogee, Champa controlled the entire central coast of what would later become Vietnam, from the Hoanh Son Pass in the north to Vung Tau in the south. Their country functioned as a loose confederation of five states named after regions of India –Indrapura (Quang Tri), Amaravati (Quang Nam), Vijaya (Binh Dinh), Kauthara (Nha Trang) and Panduranga (Phan Rang).

At the start of the 10th century, Champa came under severe pressure from Dai Viet, which was beginning its long push to the south. In 1069, Indrapura was lost to the Viets, and by 1306, Champa's northern frontier had been pushed back to the Hai Van Pass with the loss of Amaravati. The process of Vietnamese expansion proved inexorable, with Vijaya falling in 1471 and Champa – now reduced to the kingdoms of Kauthara and Panduranga – effectively a broken power. The final absorption by Vietnam was delayed until the reign of Minh Mang in 1832.

Champa disappeared – but not the Cham people. Some fled to neighbouring Cambodia, though others chose to stay under Vietnamese tutelage in their southern homelands.

The most famous mountain, which is riddles with caves, temples and paths, is **Thuy Son** (daily 7am–5pm; charge). The paths weaving through the mountain are well marked and easy to navigate. The largest mountain, Thuy Son, is home to several caves, some of which were used as Buddhist sanctuaries and even as a Viet Cong hospital. Take the second entrance on your left as you walk towards the beach. **Huyen Khong Cave** – a Buddhist sanctuary which served as a Viet Cong base – is the most spectacular. The highest cave, **Van Thong**, has a narrow passage through which you can wiggle to the top for the breathtaking views. Marble from here was used in the construction of Ho Chi Minh's tomb in Hanoi, a fact the locals are fiercely proud of. The mountains were also a haven for the Viet Cong during the war as they overlooked the vast air force base used by the Americans.

MY SON

Take road 607 south towards Hoi An, then turn west on road 608 towards Highway 1A. Travelling south from Hoi A on Highway 1A for 27km (16 miles), turn right after entering Nam Phuoc village, at the sign for My Son. Fork left after 9km (5.5 miles). This journey should take less than an hour. Buy your ticket at the mini museum and reception hall and then ride the shuttle bus about 1km (0.6 mile) to the start of the path.

The valley of **My Son** ❸ (tel: 0510-373 1757; 7am–5pm; charge), nestled under

Temple group B at My Son   *Cham woman at Po Nagar Cham towers*

Cat's Tooth Mountain, was chosen as a religious sanctuary by King Bhadravarman I, and from the fourth century, many temples and towers *(kalan)* were built in this area. These ruins are all that remains of the ancient religious capital of Amaravati, the greatest of the Cham states.

The Cham people worshipped a dual cosmology, venerating both male and female deities. In Amaravati, My Son represented the male god king, denoted by the holy Cat's Tooth Mountain and a phallic representation, the *linga* Bhadresvarain. 'Bhad' is an abbreviation of Bhadravarman, and 'esvara' refers to the Hindu god Shiva.

During the Second Indochina War (1954–75), the Viet Cong based themselves in the temples, using them as bunkers. American B52s bombed them thoroughly, leaving only a small vestige of what was once a magnificent ancient city. Traces of around 70 temples and related structures may still be found at My Son, though only about 20 are still in good condition.

Walking in a uni-directional loop, you will encounter designated temple groups: A, A', B, C, D, E and F. The additional groups, H, L and G are off-limits. The first cluster of temples which you encounter at **groups C**, **B and D** are the most intact, but the others are in various states of cataclysmic collapse. Two **meditation halls** *(mandapa)* in D have been turned into small galleries containing modest examples of sculpture, although the most interesting pieces have been carted off to

other museums. Stone phallic symbols abound throughout the temples, in the form of the male *linga* and female *yoni*. Worshipped as a symbol of the god Shiva, sacred water was poured over the *linga* and drained through the *yoni*.

After a long afternoon turn back towards Hoi An, turning east from Highway 1A on road 608, then following the river into town. Once back in Hoi An, head to the Japanese Bridge and have dinner at **The Cargo Club**, see ❷.

Food and drink

❶ BREAD OF LIFE

Dong Da Street at Bach Dang Street Roundabout; tel: 0511-356 5185; www.bread oflifedanang.com; daily B, L & D; $$
This long-standing bakery and restaurant, serving authentic American comfort food, is staffed almost entirely by the deaf. The menu includes pizza, pasta, burgers, sandwiches, elaborate breakfasts and baked macaroni. Hugely popular with expats and tourists alike.

❷ THE CARGO CLUB RESTAURANT AND HOI AN PATISSERIE

107–109 Nguyen Thai Hoc Street; tel: 0510-391 1227; www.hoianhospitality. com; daily B, L & D; $$$
Hoi An's Cargo Club offers some of the best views in town with a menu of international fare, French pastries and home-made ice cream. There is also a well-stocked wine bar.

Trag Tien Bridge

HUE'S IMPERIAL CITY

The home of the Nguyen kings, Hue's Imperial City was the seat of Vietnam's last royal dynasty. Walk through the king's gardens, royal temples and palace halls to experience at first hand the grandeur of the Nguyen Royal Court.

DISTANCE: 1.5km (1-mile) walk

TIME: A half-day

START: Trang Tien Bridge on the Perfume River

END: Hue Historical and Revolutionary Museum

POINTS TO NOTE: Hue is best reached from Hanoi or Da Nang by train. Transport to and from the citadel is most convenient by taxi. This route is best grouped with route 11. Bring an umbrella unless there is a good reason to think it won't rain, as Hue is one of the wettest cities in Vietnam. Plan to eat before or after the tour – there are no restaurants once inside the Ngo Mon. Time the route to take in one of the 30-minute shows (9.30am, 10.30am, 2.30pm and 3.30pm) at the Royal Theatre.

In 1802, after quelling the Tay Son rebellion, Lord Nguyen Phuc Anh proclaimed himself Emperor Gia Long and founded the Nguyen Dynasty. He ordered the new royal citadel to be built along the Perfume River, which became Vietnam's new capital city. Just 33 years into the dynasty's reign, the French invaded Hue. They retained the Nguyen Dynasty with nominal governance over central Vietnam and northern Vietnam. Thanks to French manipulation of the dynasty, a quick succession of emperors graced the throne, ending with Bao Dai's abdication in 1945.

ENTERING THE CITADEL

Grab a bite at **La Boulangerie Française**, see ❶, before heading north, crossing the Perfume River via **Trang Tien Bridge** ❶. Enter the citadel on the north bank. Hue's **Imperial City** (Dai Noi), including the Yellow Enclosure and Forbidden Purple City (Tu Cam Thanh), is enclosed within the all-encompassing *Kinh Thanh* (the exterior enclosure). Stone, bricks and earth were used for this wall, which was 8m (26ft) high and 20m (65ft) thick. Ten large, fortified gates, each topped with watchtowers, were built along the wall. Most of what visitors come to see today is within the Yellow Enclosure; other areas were destroyed during the Tet Offensive of 1968.

Cyclos passing by Ngo Mon

Immediately inside the first enclosure of the royal city, towards the Chuong Duc gate, are the **Nine Deities' Cannons ❷** (Sung Than Cong). The five cannons on one side represent the five elements – metal, water, wood, fire, and earth – while the other four represent the seasons.

The **Yellow Enclosure** (Hoang Thanh; daily 7am–5.30pm; charge) is the middle wall enclosing the Imperial City and its palaces, temples and flower gardens. Four richly decorated gates provided access: Ngo Mon (the southern gate, or Noon Gate), Hoa Binh (northern gate), Hien Nhon (eastern gate) and Chuong Duc (western gate).

THE NGO MON

You will enter the Imperial City through the **Ngo Mon ❸** (Noon Gate) was built of granite in 1834 during the reign of Minh Mang and is the most recognisable structure in the city. It is topped by the **Five Phoenix Watchtower** (Lau Ngu Phung).

From here, the emperors used to preside over formal ceremonies, including Emperor Bao Dai's abdication. The gate is also known as the 'Noon Gate' because the sun, representing the emperor, is at its highest at noon. It faces south and is also therefore associated with prosperity. Purchase your tickets for the citadel here.

THAI HOA PALACE

Through the Ngo Mon, walk across the Golden Water Bridge, which at one time was reserved for the emperor. It leads to **Thai Hoa Palace ❹** (Dien Thai Hoa) or 'Palace of Supreme Harmony', the most important administrative structure in the Imperial City. Here the emperor held bimonthly audiences with the court, including male members of the royal family, with civil mandarins standing before him on the left, and military mandarins on the right. The palace is in excellent condition, with its ceilings and 80 gilded beams decorated in red lacquer and gold inlay.

Kinh Thanh   D a i N o i
(Citadel)   I m p e r i a l C i t y

Trach Han

Bao Tang Tong Hop
(Hue Historical and
Revolutionary Museum)   **8**

PHU CAT   Con
Hen

Cho Dong Ba
(Market)

Nguyen Sinh Cung

Nhung

Nguyen Cong
Tru

Hoang Thanh
(Imperial
Enclosure)

Tran Hung Dao

Cau
Trang Tien

Le Loi

❶

Chua Thien Mu
(Celestial Lady
Pagoda)

Le Duan

Phu Xuan

Ngoc Binh Hotel

Cau

Hotel
Saigon Morin

Le Quy Don

Duong Ha Noi

Le Loi

Huong (Perfume)

**La Residence
Hotel and Spa**

Duong Ngo Quyen

Nguyen Hue

THANH
PHO MOI
(NEW CITY)

Dong Da

Dong Da

Duong Hung Vuong

Con Da
Vien

Bui Thi Xuan

An Cuu

Phan Dinh Phung

Notre-Dame

Cung An Dinh
(Royal Antiquities
Museum)

N

Ga Hue
(Train Station)

Phan Chu Trinh

200 m / 220 yds

Thai Hoa Palace

THE FORBIDDEN PURPLE CITY

Walking north through Thai Hoa, the **Forbidden Purple City** (Tu Cam Thanh) was reserved solely for the emperor and the royal family, who resided here behind a brick wall 4m (13ft) thick. This area was almost completely destroyed during the Tet Offensive of 1968 (the Viet Cong used the citadel as a bunker) and nearly everything that was left after that succumbed to flooding and neglect in tropical conditions.

When you first enter the area you'll find the **Left and Right Halls of the Mandarins**. The Left Hall is now devoted to photo opportunities in period costumes (charge), and the Right Hall houses an extension of the **Royal Antiquities Museum**, with small exhibits of silver, bronze, wood and writing crafts from the Nguyen Dynasty.

The **Royal Theatre** ❺ (Duyet Thi Duong), behind and to the right (east), offers 30-minute shows in the morning at 9.30 and 10.30am, and afternoons at 2.30 and 3.30pm. Performances include five or six songs and dances in elaborate customs (including lion dancers).

The emperor's **Reading Pavilion** sits behind the theatre, ornately dec-

orated with tiles, although it looks like it could collapse at any time. A number of new **covered walking corridors** have been recreated in the central field, taking significant artistic licence. In the far reaches of the expanse behind them is a pair of octagonal **Music Pavilions**.

THE TEMPLES

Return to the Thai Hoa Palace and walk west along the path to the next enclosure. The temple-shrines (*mieu*) here are dedicated to worshipping various lords and royal family members. The temple of **Trieu To Mieu** is devoted to Nguyen Kim (now used as a plant nursery), the **Thai**

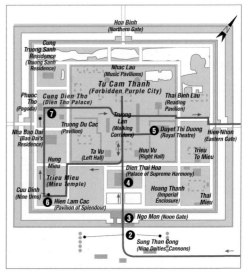

Halls of the Mandarins   *The Nine Dynastic Urns*

Mieu to Nguyen Hoang and his successors, and **Phung Tien** is a temple established to worship all of the emperors of the reigning dynasty, the **To Mieu** complex houses numerous shrines of significance as well. **Hung Mieu** is on the north side of the complex and devoted to Nguyen Phuc Luan, Gia Long's father. The well-preserved **The Mieu** houses the shrines of nine Nguyen emperors.

Also in the To Mieu complex, in front of The Mieu temple, stands the magnificently restored **Hien Lam Cac** ❻ (Pavilion of Splendour), with the **Nine Dynastic Urns** (Cuu Dinh) lined up before it.

DIEN THO PALACE

Following the signs north, the **Dien Tho Palace** ❼, built in 1804, was the traditional residence of queen mothers. It includes a bewildering 20 structures, most notably the **Phuoc Tho Pagoda**, the recent **Personal Residence of Emperor Bao Dai**, and the lovely **Truong Du Pavilion**, nestled against a small lotus pond. The beauty of the complex rivals Thai Hoa Palace.

The **Truong Sanh Residence** is a separate complex behind the palace and served as a recreation area for the queen mother.

HUE HISTORICAL AND REVOLUTIONARY MUSEUM

Exit through Hien Nhon (the eastern gate) to the nearby **Hue Historical and Revolu-** tionary Museum ❽ (Bao Tang Tong Hop; Tue–Sun 7.30–11am, 1.30–5pm; free). The central building, built in the style of a traditional *dinh* (communal house), contains a collection of local archaeological discoveries. The colonial pavilions outside are devoted to the First and Second Indochina Wars.

End the royal tour by sampling a wide selection of unique dishes at the strip of three family-run restaurants known as **Lac Thien, Lac Thanh** and **Lac Thuan**, see ❷, which can be found on the south side of the citadel.

TOMBS OF THE NGUYEN DYNASTY

Some were loved and others hated, but all the kings of Vietnam's last ruling family live on in infamy. Spend a day wandering among the monuments, gardens, lakes and chapels of the Nguyen emperors.

DISTANCE: 32km (20 miles)
TIME: A full day
START: Tu Duc's Tomb
END: Nam Giao Dan
POINTS TO NOTE: Plan to eat before or after the route, or else buy a picnic lunch from La Boulangerie Française (see route 10) to take with you. This route can be completed by a combination of car, motorbike or bicycle and boat.

The tombs of the Nguyen kings lie scattered on the hillsides along either side of the Perfume River, to the west and south of Hue. Although the dynasty had 13 kings, only seven of them reigned until their deaths, and only they are laid to rest in this valley of kings: Gia Long, Minh Mang, Thieu Tri, Tu Duc, Kien Phuc, Dong Khanh and Khai Dinh. Roads are marked with signs to the tombs. There's no one correct way to see the tombs, so if you choose to see most of them, it may require some backtracking.

TU DUC'S TOMB

Follow Bui Thi Xuan West along the Perfume River turning left (south) at the sign for the imperial tombs. The **tomb of Tu Duc ❶** is the first you will encounter, and surrounded by an onslaught of incense and souvenir shops. The mausoleum construction, begun in 1864, took three years to complete. The result resembles a royal palace in miniature and harmonises beautifully with the natural surroundings. It is perhaps the loveliest of all the Nguyen tombs and the most visited. Live traditional music is periodically performed within the tomb grounds each day for the benefit of visitors.

Tu Duc, the son of Thieu Tri and the Nguyen Dynasty's fourth king, reigned for 36 years, the longest reign of any of the Nguyen kings. He spent his leisure hours in the two pavilions beside the lake, Luu Khiem, where he wrote poetry, no doubt inspired by the beauty of his surroundings, and often went fishing. Xung Khiem is the more interesting of the two lakeside pavil-

Stone statues at the tomb of Khai Dinh

...ions. A staircase leads to the Luong Khiem mausoleum, which contains a collection of furniture, vases and jewellery boxes.

Further on is the terrace leading to the tomb, with its stone elephants, horses and mandarins. The tomb itself, ritually inaccessible, is covered by dense pine forest. The tombs of Tu Duc's adopted son, Kien Phu, and Queen Le Thien An, lie beside the lake.

THIEU TRI'S TOMB

The **tomb of Thieu Tri ❷** (daylight hours; charge) is located a few kilometres to the south along the Perfume River. Thieu Tri, Minh Mang's son, was the third Nguyen emperor and reigned from 1841–7. His tomb was built in the same elegant architectural style as his father's but on a much smaller scale, and is now crumbling. The mausoleum sprawls across several lakes and is largely open, without the surrounding walls found around other tombs.

MINH MANG'S TOMB

The **tomb of Minh Mang ❸** (daily 8am–5pm; charge) is located about 5km (3 miles) south, where the Ta Trach and Huu Trach tributaries of thePerfume River meet. Turn left (east) at the overpass and take the bridge across the river.

Minh Mang was Gia Long's fourth son and the Nguyen Dynasty's second king. Construction of the tomb was begun a year before Minh Mang's death in 1840, and was finished by his successor

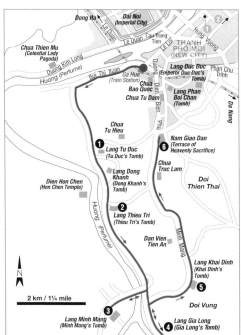

Dragon staircase in front of Khai Dinh's tomb

Thieu Tri in 1843. The setting blends the beauty of nature with the majestic architecture and superb stone sculpture created by its many anonymous craftsmen. It is at its best in mid-March, when the Trung Minh and Tan Nguyet lakes bloom with a mass of beautiful lotus flowers.

Now would be a good time to break for a picnic lunch or head back into Hue and resume the rest of the tour tomorrow.

Minh Mang was responsible for the construction of the Imperial City of Hue. He was highly respected by the Vietnamese for his reforms in the areas of customs, traditions and agriculture. However, he is disliked to this day by the Cham, as the Vietnamese ruler who dealt the last blow to the declining Champa Kingdom.

GIA LONG'S TOMB

The **tomb of Gia Long** ❹ (daily 8am–5pm; charge) is located 16km (10 miles) south from Hue. To get there from Minh Mang's tomb, cross back over to the east side of the river, head south for at least 1km (0.6 mile), and stop at the nearest boat landing to be ferried across to the tomb. The tomb sits on a hillside, and is inaccessible by road.

The tomb, begun in 1814, was completed a year after Gia Long's death in 1820. Unfortunately, the site was in the middle of a guerrilla zone during the

Vietnam War, and the tomb was considerably damaged by bombs. The tomb has been rather neglected, but the wild beauty of the site itself, with its mountainous backdrop, makes the effort to get there well worth the time.

KHAI DINH'S TOMB

About 3km (2 miles) back across the river and north on Road 49, the **tomb of Khai Dinh** ❺ (daily 8am–5pm; charge) somewhat resembles a European castle, its architecture a blend of the oriental and occidental. Made of reinforced concrete, it took 11 years to complete and was finally finished in 1931. Khai Dinh, Bao Dai's adopted father, ruled for nine years during the colonial era.

A grandiose dragon staircase leads up to the first courtyard, from where further stairs lead to a courtyard lined with stone statues of elephants, horses, and civil and military mandarins. In the centre of the courtyard stands the stele inscribed with Chinese characters composed by Bao Dai in memory of his father. The exterior lacks the tranquil charm and beauty of Minh Mang's or Tu Duc's mausoleum, and the giant dragons flanking the staircase appear rather menacing.

Once inside, however, the contrast is striking and more identifiable with the ostentatious character of the emperor. Coloured tiles pave the floor, and a huge 'dragon in the clouds' mural, painted by artists using their

The tomb of Minh Mang

feet, adorns the ceiling of the middle chamber. Bright frescoes composed of many thousands of inlaid ceramic and glass fragments depict various themes. Animals, trees and flowers provide a visual feast after the rather morbid, blackened exterior of the mausoleum.

The back room contains a small museum of the emperor's possessions, including photos, clothing, ceramics, crystal, furniture and a clock. A life-size bronze statue of Khai Dinh, made in France in 1922, rests on a dais on top of the tomb.

NAM GIAO DAN

Head about 4km (2.5 miles) south on Dien Bien Phu (also known as Minh Mang Street or road 49 here) to **Nam Giao Dan** ❻ (Terrace of Heavenly Sacrifice; daylight hours recommended; free), an esplanade surrounded by a park of pines and conifers and one of the less visited of Hue's attractions. Built by Gia Long in 1802, in its day it was considered a very sacred and solemn place.

Composed of three terraces – two square and one circular – the esplanade represents the union of sky and earth. Every three years the Nam Giao (Festival of Sacrifice) took place at the centre of the circular platform. From here the emperor, worshipped as a god himself, would arrange to have a buffalo sacrificed to the god of the sky,

who is believed to govern the destiny of the world.

With today's tour finished, head north 2km (1.5 miles) on Dien Bien Phu, then right on Le Loi to Hue's commercial centre for dinner at **La Carambole**, see ❶, or **Tropical Garden**, see ❷.

General Post Office on the shore of Hoam Kiem Lake

HANOI: ART AND ARCHITECTURE

The political and cultural capital of Vietnam, Hanoi is one of Asia's loveliest cities, with tree-lined, history-drenched boulevards. Stroll around Vietnam's urban lake, delight in French Colonial architecture and browse the nation's best museums.

DISTANCE: Day 1: walk 5km (3.5 miles), drive 4km (2.5 miles); Day 2: walk 3km (2 miles), drive: 12km (7.5 miles)

TIME: 2 days

START: Day 1: Monument to Le Thai To; Day 2: Temple of Literature

END: Day 1: National Museum of Vietnamese History; Day 2: Vietnam Museum of Ethnology

POINTS TO NOTE: This route can be combined with route 13. Many attractions and services close at lunchtime, and several museums close on Mondays. Those who wish to take a guided tour of Hanoi's art history can also consider Sophie's Art Tour (www.sophiesarttour.com)

Hanoi's development may lag behind other Asian capitals, but this is good news for most visitors. Despite increasingly evident signs of development, the city still retains its unique identity, with a collection of legend-strewn lakes, low-rise colonial buildings and ancient pagodas. Glittering skyscrapers and shopping malls are moving in, but they are not dominating the city centre.

Downtown Hanoi, which contains Hanoi's main areas of interest, is relatively small, with a distinct provincial feel. This makes travelling around the city relatively easy. There are many interesting must-sees, but Hanoi's main draw is its ambience and street life, a drama that unfolds daily on the streets, and in temples and markets. The best way to appreciate this mesmerising city is on foot, but you will need to make plenty of stops given the cluttered pavements and intense traffic. Take your time to savour its captivating sights, absorbing the sounds and aromas found at every corner you take.

HOAN KIEM LAKE

Begin your tour at 8am; breakfast is taken en route. Your starting point is the north end of Le Thai To Street, at the northwest tip of **Hoan Kiem Lake**. The Lake of the Restored Sword (Ho

Rising Sun Bridge

Hoan Kiem) is steeped in legend. In the 15th century, Emperor Le Thai To was supposedly handed a magic sword by a divine turtle living in the lake, helping him repel Chinese invaders. After the country had been liberated, the turtle snatched back the sword and disappeared into the lake – hence the name. This same, highly endangered species of turtle lives in the lake. Hoan Kiem was once part of the Red River and a deep swamp, the surrounding area comprising marshland and small lakes, ringed with stilt houses and dotted with small islands, until the French drained the land in the 19th century. Have a traditional noodle soup breakfast at the small, traditional **Pho Thin Bo Ho** tucked down an alley at 61 Dinh Tien Hoang, see ❶. Next, head south down Le Thai To Street. To your right, inside the **Monument to Le Thai To** ❶ is a statue of Emperor Le Thai To and to your left, on an islet in the lake, the three-tiered, 18th-century **Turtle Tower** ❷ (Thap Rua).

As you continue your walk, you will pass the small tower called **Hoa Phuong** opposite the **General Post Office** (Buu Dien Ha Noi). The tower was once an entrance to a pagoda. Around the southern tip of the lake, **Ly Thai To Gardens** featured a giant statue of the former emperor of the same name.

The austere, Soviet-style **Hanoi People's Committee Building** (to the right) stands in sharp contrast to the delicately arched, red-lacquered wooden **Rising Sun Bridge** (The Huc), leading to the **Ngoc Son Temple** ❸ (Den Ngoc Son), also known as the 'Temple of the Jade Mound' (daily 8am–6pm; charge). The temple is mainly associated with Tran Hung Dao, the general who defeated the Mongols at the Bach Dang River in 1279. The temple was part of a 15th-century complex of palaces, pagodas and temples, dedicated to national heroes. What remains today are mostly 19th-century buildings, one displaying a preserved giant turtle that lived in the lake. The live Hoan Kiem Lake Turtle *(Rafetus leloii)* is still regularly spotted here causing the traffic around the lake to come to a halt as people jump off motorbikes to snap a photo.

HANOI'S OLD QUARTER

Walk north up **Ho Hoan Kiem Street** to get to Cau Go Street. Across the road is **Hang Be Market** ❹. This is a good place to get street-food snacks, like Hanoi's famous sweet black beans and yogurt. Walk through the market, turn left and exit on **Dinh Liet Street** – the start of Hanoi's most famous sight, the Old Quarter.

The **Old Quarter** (Pho Phuong) is an ancient merchants' quarter which evolved in the 13th century when 36 artisans' guilds concentrated around the Citadel to serve the court. Each of the 36 streets was named according to the merchandise on offer, for example,

Hang Ma Street in the Old Quarter

Hang (merchandise) or *Buom* (sails). Today, many streets have changed their wares, but some still specialise in the original craft.

The Old Quarter still retains many 'tube houses', so called because of their narrow facades and long length. These single-storey shops belie their depth, containing dwellings at the rear and tiny courtyards. Feudal laws taxed shops according to their width – explaining why many are less than 3m (10ft) wide

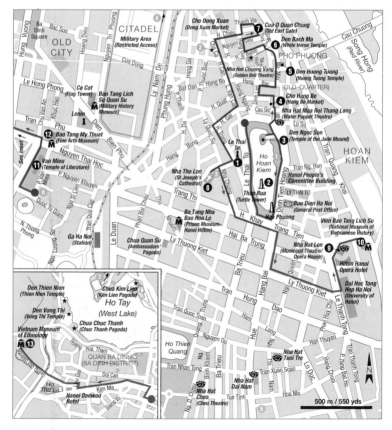

Traditional shopping *The Old Quarter is home to many craft shops*

– and decreed buildings should be no higher than a passing royal palanquin, in deference to the emperor. Over the years, many buildings incorporated Western influences, like balconies and additional floors.

Walk along Dinh Liet and turn right into Hang Bac, one of Hanoi's oldest streets. *Bac* means silver, and silversmiths originally settled here casting silver bars and coins. Today, shops still sell silver. At the intersection with Dinh Liet and Ta Hien streets, the **Golden Bell Theatre** (Nha Hat Chuong Vang) – a traditional Vietnamese theatre – was once the Hanoi Imperial Guards' headquarters.

At the end of Hang Bac, gravestone workshops spill out onto the pavements. Head into **Ma May** (Rattan Street). Members of the notorious Chinese Black Flag Army – peasant mercenaries from southern China – once lived here. In the 19th century, they helped the Vietnamese fight wars against various clans and the French. Near here, a tributary once ran parallel to Hang Buom (Sails Street), enabling boats to sail up here to buy nautical supplies. When the French filled in the To Lich River, merchants switched to selling imported goods and dried foodstuffs, still sold today.

The Old Quarter's most noteworthy antique house is **No. 87**. This former Communal House (Gioi Thieu Nha Co So), beautifully restored to its late 19th-century condition, is open to the public (daily 8.30am–5.30pm; charge). The restored **No. 69**, now transformed into the **69 Bar-Restaurant**, once had a secret tunnel used by resistance fighters running through its walls. Don't miss **Huong Tuong Temple ❺** (Den Huong Tuong) at No. 64, founded in 1450 (open on festival days and 1st and 15th days of the lunar month; 9–11am, 3–7pm; free).

White Horse Temple ❻ (Den Bach Ma), at No. 76 Hang Buom Street, is the Old Quarter's most revered and ancient place of worship, its architecture influenced by the Chinese community (daily 8–11am, 2–5pm). Founded in 1010 and restored many times, this stunning temple honours the white horse that appeared to Emperor Ly Thai To in a dream. For several decades this National Heritage Site doubled as a storage house and printing workshop. During the fight for independence from French rule, many resistance fighters hid in the temple.

Turn right into **Hang Giay** (Paper Street) – with dilapidated buildings crammed with goods – and into **Nguyen Sieu Street**. Hanoi's first inhabitants settled along the banks of the To Lich River, which flowed where this street now runs. **Co Luong Temple** (Den Co Luong) is at No. 28, its entrance flanked by two colourful guards.

Now pass along **Dao Duy Tu Street**, with its row of old houses, to reach **Old East Gate ❼** (Cua O Quan Chong) – the only city gate to remain from the origi-

nal 16 that once marked the city's entry points. To your left is **Thanh Ha Street**, a fascinating alley lined with market and food stalls. Follow it round, until you reach **Hang Chieu** (Mat Street), which turns into Hang Ma (Paper Votive Street) – a mass of red, with lanterns and paper votive offerings used for Buddhist ceremonies. Turn south down Cha Ca Street, stopping at No. 14 for lunch at **Cha Ca La Vong**, see ❷.

THE FRENCH QUARTER

Grab a taxi, cyclo, moto driver or simply walk south on Cha Ca Street, then right on Hang Gai for a shopping diversion in the boutique shops, continued with a left on Hang Trong, and then right (west) to Nha Tho Street, behind the ANZ Bank. Consider a break for iced lemon tea at one of the many small places that line the cathedral square or opt for the retro themed **Cong Ca Phe** at 27 Nha Tho, see ❸.

St Joseph's Cathedral
Sitting at the west end of the street, **St Joseph's Cathedral** ❽ (Nha Tho Lon) is the one of the French Quarter's oldest buildings and Hanoi's only Gothic structure (closed noon–2pm for lunch). It was built by the French on the site of ancient Bao Thien Pagoda – demolished to make way for the cathedral – and consecrated on Christmas night in 1886. Many visitors have remarked that the Catholic cathedral resembles a smaller version of Paris's Notre-Dame. Inside are beautiful stained-glass windows and an altar decorated with gold leaf. Regular masses are usually packed, and at Christmas and Easter Vietnamese-style biblical scenes are mounted on the front facade.

Opera House area
Next, wander down to the intersection of Ly Thuong Kiet Street and Le Thanh Tong Street. As you head north, note the impressive 1920s building at the corner, which houses the medical annexe of the University of Hanoi, the former University of Indochina.

Le Thanh Tong and its surrounding streets are full of colonial villas housing diplomatic residences and embassies, but the most magnificent structure is the **Opera House** ❾, or Municipal Theatre (Nha Hat Lon), on the corner of Trang Tien Street. Built by the French (modelled on the neo-Baroque Paris Opera), it opened in 1911 to keep the colonials entertained (and remind them of home). Restored to its former grandeur and reopened in 1997, the Opera House is stunning, with a sweeping marble staircase, crystal chandeliers and red and gold leaf decor. Unfortunately, there are no tours or access, unless you have tickets for a cultural performance (details posted outside and at the ticket kiosk just inside). On 19 August 1945, the Viet Minh declared an independent

Hanoi's Opera House

democratic republic from the balcony of the Opera House, unfurling their banners in the process. Bullet holes from hand-to-hand fighting are still visible in the Hall of Mirrors inside. There are a number of coffee shops and bars in the area that make good rest stops as well as ice cream shops just across the way on Trang Tien Street. Adjacent to the Opera House is the luxury **Hilton Hanoi Opera Hotel**, with a pleasing facade that replicates the style of the Opera House. The interior, however, is very modern.

National Museum of Vietnamese History

Turn right into Trang Tien Street, walking five minutes towards the freeway, to visit the **National Museum of Vietnamese History** ❿ (Vien Bao Tang Lich Su Vietnam; tel: 04-3824 1384; daily 8am–4.30pm; charge). This stunning, renovated building, typifying hybrid Indochinese architecture, houses one of the city's best museums. It has easy-to-follow displays, surprisingly low propaganda content and excellent archaeological and historical relics. Displays include ancient Dong Son bronze drums, Neolithic grave relics and clothes and artefacts belonging to the Nguyen emperors. Relics located in the grounds include the oldest epitaph in Southeast Asia, written in Sanskrit.

If time allows, make a diversion by taxi to **Manzi**, see ❶, at 14 Phan Huy Ich for a coffee at this cafe and gallery space which shows the work of both local and international artists.

Finish your day with dinner at **Chim Sao**, see ❺, a little to the south on Ngo Hue street.

TEMPLE OF LITERATURE

The **Temple of Literature** ⓫ (Van Mieu; summer daily 7.30am–5pm, winter daily 8am–5pm; charge) was founded in 1070 as Vietnam's principal Confucian sanctuary and to honour Vietnamese scholars. In 1076 Vietnam's first university, the National Academy (Quoc Tu Giam), was established here to educate future mandarins in Confucian doctrine. Despite the capital moving to Hue in 1802, examinations continued until the early 20th century, before the French put a stop to them.

An oasis of calm and beauty, the ground plan is modelled on the birthplace of Confucius, with five interconnecting walled courtyards, complete with gateways and lotus ponds. In the third courtyard, 82 stone stelae, mounted on tortoises, are inscribed with the names of 1,307 laureates of state examinations held at the National Academy from 1442–1779. The fourth courtyard holds the main temple buildings – a red-lacquered **House of Ceremonies and Sanctuary**, dedicated to Confucius. The fifth, final courtyard once housed the National Academy buildings; unfortunately these were

Temple of Literature

destroyed by French bombs in 1947 and replaced since with a new two-storey pavilion. Traditional music recitals are performed here, subject to demand (and a small contribution).

VIETNAM FINE ARTS MUSEUM

The **Vietnam Fine Arts Museum** ⑫ (Bao Tang My Thuat), a five-minute walk away, is north of Van Mieu at 66 Nguyen Thai Hoc Street (tel: 04-3823 3084; daily 8am–5pm; charge). The museum holds around 14,000 artworks from the prehistoric to the present. Highlights include a multi-armed bodhisattva statue, 18th-century wooden Buddhist statues and some impressive folk art, including ancestral worship pictures on a handcrafted paper called *do*. Most of the displays concentrate on the development of Vietnamese art from the 20th century to the present through paintings and sculpture – silk and lacquer are given special emphasis.

After the museum, enjoy lunch at **Koto** (59 Van Mieu Street), a social enterprise restaurant across the street from the Temple of Literature, see ⑥.

Vietnam Museum of Ethnology

Take a taxi to the far west side of town (about 20 minutes from the Fine Arts Museum) to the **Vietnam Museum of Ethnology** ⑬ (Bao Tang Dan Toc Hoc Vietnam, Nguyen Van Huyen Road; tel: 04-3756 2193; www.vme.org.vn; Tue–Sun 8.30am–5.30pm; charge) is perhaps Vietnam's most progressive museum. This museum was officially opened in 1997 by French President Jacques Chirac and designed with the help of the Musée de l'Homme in Paris. It is the finest of all of Vietnam's ethnic museums.

As a centre for research and conservation, the museum serves to promote a greater understanding of Vietnam's 54 ethnic minority groups. If you haven't the time to visit these ethnic groups, the museum is the next best thing to understand their diverse heritage, cultures and lifestyles. The museum has gathered nearly 15,000 ethnic artefacts from across Vietnam, including musical instruments, masks, baskets and garments, as well as maps, wall charts and photographs, which are superbly showcased. Dioramas depict scenes such as conical hat production, markets and various ritual ceremonies – illustrated by audiovisual tapes. There is even a reconstruction of a traditional Black Thai house. Check the boards outside the main entrance for information on daily water puppet shows. You will also find a permanent display of authentic, life-size minority dwellings, as well as a grave house behind the museum building.

After a long and leisurely visit through the extensive museum, take a taxi to **Cousins**, see ⑦, at 3 Quang Ba on the shore of West Lake (Ho Tay) for a leisurely european al fresco meal.

Fine Arts Museum

Food and drink

❶ PHO THIN BO HO

61 Dinh Tien Hoang; no phone; daily B, L
& D; $

A classic example of a no-nonsense Hanoi
pho stall, selling the staple Hanoian
breakfast of beef noodle soup. if you haven't
tried it yet, now's the time.

❷ CHA CA LA VONG

14 Cha Ca Street; tel: 04-3825 3929; daily
B, L & D; $$$

One of Hanoi's most famous dishes, *cha
ca* is the only thing served here – fish
grilled on a clay brazier at your table – with
rice noodles, peanuts and herbs. Perhaps
due to its fame, the service at this long-
established eatery has become rather surly
over the years, but the history of the place
means it's still worth a visit for many.

❸ CONG CA PHE

27 Nha Tho Street; tel: 04-3762 2645;
www.congcaphe.com; daily B, L & D; $

This is one of the many communist era/
military themed Cong Ca Phes that have
sprung up around the capital since the first
one opened on Trieu Viet Vuong (aka coffee
street). Try the excellent yoghurt coffee and
grab a seat outside to enjoy the cathedral
views.

❹ MANZI

14 Phan Huy Ich; tel: 04-3710 3397;
http://facebook.com/manzihanoi

Run by the welcoming Tram and Bill, Manzi
is an art space and café in one showing
the work of local and international artists.
Excellent, strong Vietnamese coffee and a
good line in cakes.

❺ CHIM SAO

65 Ngo Hue Street; tel: 04-3970633;
www.chimsao.com; daily L & D; $$

Take off your shoes and ascend the stairs
to take a seat on the floor and enjoy
traditional Vietnamese dishes from the
north including excellent sautéed duck,
buffalo and frog, superb banana flower
salad and fantastic sticky rice. The rice
wine menu is long and lethal.

❻ KOTO

59 Van Mieu Street; tel: 04-3747 0337;
www.koto.com.au; daily B, L & D; $$$

Koto serves tasty international food:
the Mediterranean wraps and paninis,
lemongrass chicken skewers, spring
rolls and buffet breakfast are all
recommended. Koto is a non-profit project
providing hospitality training for Hanoi's
disadvantaged youth.

❼ COUSINS

6 Quang Ba, Tay Ho District; tel: 0123 867
0098; daily B, L & D; $$$$

On the shore of West Lake, Cousins has
quickly made a name for itself by serving
an innovative range of European dishes
including grills and pastas. Take a peaceful
seat outside and enjoy a glass of sangria.

Mausoleum of Ho Chi Minh

HANOI: HO CHI MINH'S LEGACY

A full-day route which takes in the heart of Hanoi's political and diplomatic centre, including Ho Chi Minh's mausoleum, museum, stilt house and the One Pillar Pagoda. Explore the legacy left by the father of modern Vietnam.

DISTANCE: 5.5km (3.5 miles)
TIME: A full day
START: Ba Dinh Square
END: Thanh Long Water Puppet Theatre
POINTS TO NOTE: This route is for history buffs; it is unlikely to grab the interest of children. As an exploration of Hanoi, it can be combined with route 12. Transport is available within the city in the form of taxis and motorbikes.

While wandering the world, a young Vietnamese revolutionary, Nguyen Ai Quoc, better known as Ho Chi Minh, developed a strong sense of political consciousness. Ho Chi Minh, or Uncle Ho as he is known locally, became the famous Marxist revolutionary who helped secure Vietnam's independence. Today much of his ideology has been forgotten, but his image remains as cherished as ever: his face is on every banknote, the nation's capital is named after him and nearly every town has a statue of him. Unravelling the man behind the myth is difficult: Ho Chi

Minh was only one of several pseudonyms he used and he rarely gave interviews; even his birthday is disputed.

Ho founded the Indochinese Communist Party in Guangzhou, China, in 1930. He lived in the USA and the UK before heading to France, where he studied communism and began calling for the French to leave his homeland. After studying further in the Soviet Union and China, he returned to Vietnam in 1941 to fight the French. After 30 years in self-imposed exile, Ho Chi Minh finally walked back across the border into Vietnam in 1941 and co-founded the League for the Independence of Vietnam (Viet Minh). His goal was not only independence from French colonial rule and Japanese occupation, but also 'the union of diverse nationalist groups under Communist direction'.

Ho formed the National Liberation Committee and called for an uprising, the August Revolution, after which the north and the rest of Vietnam came under Viet Minh control. On 2 September 1945, Ho established the Democratic Republic of Vietnam with his

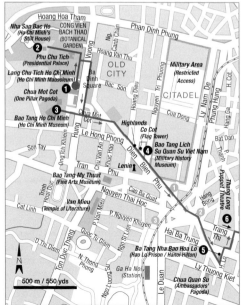

Soldiers on patrol

Declaration of Independence Speech in Ba Dinh Square, near where he would later lie in state. This date became Vietnam's National Day and was also to be the date of Ho's death.

After decades of war with the French and then the Americans, the 1973 Paris Accord provided a ceasefire and a withdrawal of US troops. However, Ho Chi Minh had already died in 1969 without seeing his vision of a unified Vietnam become a reality.

Regardless of one's own personal feelings about his legacy, there is no denying that Ho Chi Minh didn't merely have a strong influence, but is directly responsible for the reshaping and unification of modern Vietnam. Here in Hanoi his legacy is most evident, with the the the country's greatest monument, mausoleum and museum dedicated in his honour.

BA DINH SQUARE

Eat breakfast prior to departure and take a taxi to the Ho Chi Minh Mausoleum, passing the Vietnam Military History Museum, Cot Co Flag Tower (a remnant of the Citadel) and Highlands Café en route. Aim to be at your starting point – 8 Hung Vuong Street, near Chua Mot Cot Street, at Ba Dinh Square – by 8.30am.

The difference between the Old Quarter's fascinating chaos and **Ba Dinh Square** could not be more contrasting. Huge, austere Ba Dinh Square, with its Soviet-style architecture, is a sobering reminder of where you are – a socialist republic. This site of pilgrimage is where the former president of the Democratic Republic of Vietnam and founder of the Vietnamese Communist Party – Ho Chi Minh

Presidential Palace

– lies for eternity in a massive, stark mausoleum (just like comrades Mao, Lenin and Stalin). In this very spot, Ho Chi Minh read out his Declaration of Independence on 2 September 1945: today, military parades and ceremonies occasionally take place here, watched by high-ranking party and government officials. Opposite the mausoleum the gigantic new National Assembly Building designed by GMP Architekten now stands competes for attention.

Walk along **Chua Mot Cot Street**, towards the intersection with **Dien Bien Phu Street**. French architectural influence is never far away; a prime example is the impressive **Ministry of Foreign Affairs** building. More fine examples of Alpine-style colonial buildings – housing embassies and diplomatic residences – are located at the top of Dien Bien Phu Street.

Colonial villas frame the square's northern boundary. Back at the square, on your left is the old **National Assembly Hall** and beyond this, the **Heroes' Memorial**. You may catch the Changing of the Guard ceremony outside the mausoleum entrance, which usually takes place on the hour.

HO CHI MINH MAUSOLEUM

The **Ho Chi Minh Mausoleum** ❶ (Lang Chu Tich Ho Chi Minh) was built by the Soviet Union as a gift to the Vietnamese (Apr–Oct Tue–Thur 7.30–10.30am, Sat–Sun 7.30–11am, Nov–Mar Tue– Thur 8–11am, Sat–Sun 8–11.30am; free). It was inaugurated on 29 August 1975 (although Ho Chi Minh died in 1969). At the arrival point, leave your bags and personal effects such as cameras and mobile phones at the designated cloakroom or at the 'collection points' nearby (but do hold on to your wallet/purse). Remember to collect your belongings before these close at 11am. Pass through security control and under the intimidating gaze of soldier guards; queue in strict line.

As you enter the mausoleum, it's prudent to stop talking or laughing, take your hands out of your pockets (and take off your hat if you're wearing one) and adopt a respectful demeanour. If you forget, the guards will certainly remind you. Inside a cold room, you will slowly file past Ho Chi Minh's embalmed body lying in a glass casket.

Ho Chi Minh's Mausoleum closes for 'maintenance' sometime during September to November. In the past, at this time, the body was packed off to Russia for re-embalming, much like Lenin's own corpse. Apparently this is now undertaken in Hanoi. It's ironic that the egalitarian, unassuming Ho lies in a huge memorial; supposedly his last wish was to be cremated. However, given the reverence for the 'forefather of modern Vietnam', this wasn't considered a feasible option. Foreigners may find this whole process strange, but for most Vietnamese, paying respect to 'Uncle Ho' is a sacred task.

The Ho Chi Minh Museum   *One Pillar Pagoda*

PRESIDENTAL PALACE AND HO CHI MINH'S STILT HOUSE

Exit the other side, where you are ushered to the next part of the grounds, **Ho Chi Minh's Memorial Site** (summer 7.30–11am, 2–4pm, winter 8–11am, 1.30–4pm; charge) inside the Presidential Palace area.

The Presidential Palace
Walk through the wooded gardens, passing the magnificent **Presidential Palace**. Unless you have an invitation, this is the nearest you'll get to the restored colonial building, as it is closed to the public. Built in 1906, this was home to several governor-generals of Indochina and is now used by the president. For the last 15 years of his life, Ho used the Presidential Palace for government council and receiving guests, but because of his simple lifestyle, he refused to reside here.

Ho Chi Minh's Stilt House
Ho Chi Minh lived in two unassuming houses on the grounds instead. The first (along with a garage with his cars) is on your left (access isn't possible, but peeks through the windows are), and the other, a specially constructed stilt house further to your right, beside a picturesque carp pond.
Ho Chi Minh's Stilt House 2 (Nha San Bac Ho) was where Ho worked and lived from 1958–69. Beautifully preserved with varnished wood and split

bamboo screens, the modestly furnished quarters consist of an upstairs study and bedroom, plus an open, ground-floor meeting room. It was in a rear building that Ho passed away on 2 September 1969. Vietnam is clearly intent on preserving not just Ho's body, but also his personal items, as everything from his furniture to his pens are here. There is even a garage housing his Peugeot 404.

HO CHI MINH MUSEUM AND ONE PILLAR PAGODA

Walk south on Hung Vuong Street, past the mausoleum to the Ho Chi Minh Museum compound, which also houses the One Pillar Pagoda.

The Ho Chi Minh Museum
The **Ho Chi Minh Museum 3** (Bao Tang Ho Chi Minh) is a massive angular, Soviet-style monstrosity (tel: 04-3846 3752; daily 8–11.30am, 2–4pm, except Mon, and Fri pm; charge). Dominating the tiny One Pillar Pagoda, the museum opened on 19 May 1990 (the 100th anniversary of Ho Chi Minh's birth). It celebrates Ho's revolutionary life, especially his exile years, and the pivotal role he played in Vietnam's history in the context of international communist development.

As you walk through the unidirectional museum you will encounter exhibits of photos, documents and personal effects, such as his rubber san-

Military History Museum

dals, walking stick and the disguise he used to flee Hong Kong. The exhibition departs from tradition with a surprisingly modern, almost surreal touch. Bizarre symbolic installations feature giant artificial fruit on enormous, lopsided furniture, a brick volcano and even a totem pole. Try figuring out the symbolism!

One Pillar Pagoda

The **One Pillar Pagoda** (Chua Mot Cot) is one of Hanoi's most recognised symbols. Originally built in 1049 by King Ly Thai Thong, this unique wooden pagoda rests on a single concrete pillar rising out of a murky green pool – it is supposed to symbolise the sacred lotus sprouting from the waters of suffering. It is said the king saw a goddess who, while seated on a lotus flower, handed him a male heir. The king later married a peasant girl who gave him a son, and the pagoda was built in gratitude for the premonition. The pillar is a late 1950s replacement after French soldiers blew up the original structure in 1954. Prime Minister Nehru of India planted the banyan tree behind the pagoda in 1958 during an official visit to the then fledgling Vietnamese republic.

MILITARY HISTORY MUSEUM AND FLAG TOWER

Cross to the east side of Ba Dinh Square then south on Dien Bien Phu Street, arriving at the nearby **Military History Museum ❹** (Bao Tang Lich Su Quan Su Viet Nam; 28A Dien Bien Phu Street; tel: 04-3823 4264; 8–11.30am, 1–4.30pm, closed Mon and Fri; charge). The museum traces the development of Vietnam's armed forces through 30 galleries, from battles with the Mongols and Chinese, all the way up through America and the Khmer Rouge. Outside you'll see captured fighter planes, tanks and other military equipment.

Prior to visiting the museum, wander down the road for lunch at **The Kafe**, see ❶, or take a light lunch at the **Highlands Coffee** next door. Beside the museum, the **Cot Co** (Flag Tower) is the only part of Emperor Gia Long's Citadel that is open to the public. Admission is free, so climb to the top for a fantastic view of the city.

HOA LO PRISON

Take a taxi or walk southeast on Dien Bien Phu Street, continuing down Tho Nhuom Street. Then take a left on Hoa Lo Street, arriving at **Hoa Lo Prison ❺** (tel: 04-3824 6358; daily 8–11.30am, 1.30–4.30pm; charge). Opened in 1896, this walled prison compound once occupied an entire block. Known back then as Maison Centrale, it was the largest French prison in North Vietnam at the time. A small section now remains, preserved as a museum.

Most of the museum concentrates on the plight of countless Vietnamese patriots and revolutionaries imprisoned and tortured here under French

Hoa Lo Prison exhibit

rule, pre-1954. Many grim, authentic relics remain, including instruments of torture, fetters, death-row cells and the guillotine – the way many inmates met their tragic deaths.

Towards the back, two fascinating rooms document the capture, incarceration and subsequent release of American POWs through a collection of photographs, documents and attire. Hanoi's notorious prison was dubbed the 'Hanoi Hilton' by US POWs incarcerated here during the war. These included Douglas Pete Peterson, the first US Ambassador to the Socialist Republic of Vietnam, and former presidential hopeful and US senator John McCain, who bailed out into Truc Bach Lake.

DINNER AND WATER PUPPETS

Enjoy pizza at **Net Hue**, see ❷, or wander to **Ray Quan**, see ❸, on Nguyen Khuyen Street to dine on Vietnamese food right on the train tracks that cut through the city.

After dinner, head to the **Thang Long Water Puppet Theatre** ❻ (Nha Hat Mua Roi Thang Long; tel: 04-3825 5450; www.thanglongwaterpuppet.org) at 57 Dinh Tien Hoang Street on Hoan Kiem Lake. Water puppetry is one of the oldest indigenous forms of entertainment in Vietnam. Wooden puppets play out stories based on fables as well as historical and daily events. The light-hearted performance is a good way to unwind after a day of ideology and war.

Food and drink

❶ THE KAFE

18 Dien Bien Phu Street; tel: 04-6680 2770; www.kafefood.com.vn; daily L & D; $$$$

There are now a few Kafes around town, but this is the original. Run by a Vietnamese-German, it takes inspiration from Jamie Oliver and combines it with some Vietnamese flavours. Try the excellent pork chops and the carrot and apple juice. Very popular with the younger Hanoian crowd.

❷ NET HUE

198 Hang Bong Street; tel: 091 2587887; www.nethue.com.vn; B, L, D; $-$$

Part of a small chain of Hue restaurants that has expanded in Hanoi thanks to the superb cuisine on offer, on a par with the food you will find in Hue city itself. Order as much as you can and share dishes. Don't miss the 'che' desserts – try the banana version.

❸ RAY QUAN

8A Nguyen Khuyen; tel: 09-1357 8588; daily L & D; $$

Not the easiest of restaurants to find, Ray Quan is hidden along the railway tracks making getting here a mini adventure in itself. A range of Vietnamese dishes come well prepared and the rice wine list is the most varied in town. Try the Vit Xao Ray – the house style sautéed duck.

THE PERFUME PAGODA

A day trip to the ethereal homeland of Buddhism in Vietnam, the Perfume Pagoda, is one of the highlights of Hanoi. The boat ride alone is worth the trip, but the hike to the 'most beautiful temple under the southern sky' is the grand finale.

DISTANCE: A 120km (74-mile) return drive southwest of Hanoi, followed by a 3-hour return boat ride, and finally a 4km (2.5-mile) return hike.

TIME: A full day

START/END: Yen Vi Village Boat Pier on the Yen River

POINTS TO NOTE: Don't make this trip during weekends and festivals, in order to avoid crowds. Identical organised tours, sold by every hotel and ticket office in Hanoi, are the easiest way to reach the Perfume Pagoda, though this eliminates the option of visiting other temples or grottoes in the area. The route requires considerable walking up steep inclines. Children and the elderly especially may wish to use the optional gondola instead.

The site of the oddly misnamed **Perfume Pagoda** (Chua Huong; daily 7.30am–6pm; charge) comprises a group of temples covering an area of 30 sq km (11.5 sq miles). Built into the limestone cliffs of the 'Ancient Vestiges of Perfume Grotto' (Dong Huong Tich), otherwise known as the Perfume Mountains, the earliest temples date from the 15th century. By the early 20th century there were over 100. This area was the site for some bitter uprisings against the French colonialists and as a result, several temples were destroyed during the late 1940s. Fortunately, the area retains much of its natural splendour and is regarded as one of the most beautiful spots in Vietnam.

During the first two months after Tet (roughly February/March or March/April depending on the lunar calendar), the Perfume Pagoda can get very crowded with pilgrims, making for a frustrating (or alternatively, highly interesting) experience. The walk up the mountain is steep and can be quite tough going, so wear sensible shoes and bring a bottle of water. In the summer, it can get very hot and sweaty. Boats have no cover, so wear sun protection. As there are

Boat ride on the Yen River to the Perfume Pagoda

no places to eat along the way, bring a picnic lunch if your tour package does not include one, plus a torch for the caves.

THE BOAT RIDE

The journey by road south from Hanoi brings you to riverside **Yen Vi village** ❶, where you board a shallow metal-bottomed boat (there are no roads to the Perfume Pagoda). For many, the 90-minute boat trip along the wide, swiftly flowing **Yen River** is almost as worthwhile as visiting the pagoda itself. Here fishermen wade the crystal waters among floating graves of their ancestors. As the oarsman steers the boat along the river, relax and take in the mesmerising landscape of jagged limestone hills.

THE MOUNTAIN HIKE

Disembark from the boat at the base of the Huong Tich Mountains for your 1.5–2-hour hike. **Thien Tru Temple** ❷ or Heavenly Kitchen (a reference to a Vietnamese constellation, not the secular noodle stalls that cluster around it) reaches up the mountain ahead. Most groups will have lunch at the **food stalls**, see ❶, here. From here, weary travellers can take the convenient **cable car** ❸ (*cap treo*; charge) or continue up the path to the right of the temple, which leads to the destination 2km (1.25 miles) away. On your return, you may wish to climb the stone staircase to the right of the path leading to the Tien **Son Temple** ❹, where there are unusual stone musical instruments made from stalagmites.

After 10 minutes along the main path, you will see a shrine built over a spring. Legend has it that if you bathe in **Giai Oan** ❺, your spirit will be purified and false charges against you cleared. Where the path thins and becomes a little steeper, you will see the shrine for the **'Goddess of the Mountains'** ❻ (Cua Vong). Your destination lies just below the summit of this mountain.

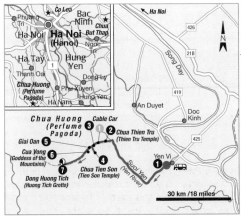

In Huong Tich Grotto

HUONG TICH GROTTO

You will see the portal and 120 stone steps bedecked with Buddhist flags leading down to the smoky depths of **Huong Tich Grotto** ➐. Chinese characters etched on the outside of the cave in 1770 declare this to be the 'most beautiful grotto under the southern sky'. Romantically inclined Vietnamese compare the cave to a dragon's mouth, with the steps leading into the cavern as its throat.

The huge stalagmites at the mouth of the cave bear curious names. The bulbous one in the centre is called the **Rice Stack**, while other stalagmites inside have been named the **Mountain of the Teenage Goddess**, **Silkworms Chamber**, **Cocoons Rack** and the **Heap of Coins**. The bell near the entrance dates from 1655 and is only beaten on ceremonial occasions.

Food and drink

① FOOD STALLS
Located at the boat pier; daily B, L & D; $$
There are a dozen humble food stalls located at the boat landing on the base of Huong Tich Mountain. Usually a group lunch at a stall of the guide's choosing is part of package tours. Food is local fare (mostly stir-fried vegetables and fried fish) with rice. Drinks cost extra.

ALTARS, INCENSE AND STATUES

As your eyes grow accustomed to the darkness you will see many altars and statues of deities twinkling with candlelight. The central one houses an important statue of **Quan Am** (Goddess of Mercy), the female personification of the Buddha. Her androgynous figure is swathed in a diaphanous fabric. According to folklore, the bodhisattva Avalokiteshvara transformed himself into the female deity Quan Am here, and the shrine is dedicated to her. Through the haze of incense smoke you will see women with offerings of fruit and incense. Many barren women come to pray for children from the goddess inside.

For many Vietnamese this is the most important religious area in the whole of Vietnam, and many devout Buddhists will try to visit the shrine at least once in their lives. It is said that the Buddha himself may have visited this area once, leaving his 'perfumed footprint', the first of many theories about the origins of the name 'Perfume'.

Today, monks still conduct services on request. If you come across one, listen for the soothing pitter-patter of Buddhist drums keeping time with the sound of condensation droplets falling in the cave.

For your return journey, choose a nice spot on the boat to enjoy the scenery that has inspired generations of Vietnamese poets and monks.

Sa Pa's Catholic chapel

SA PA

A former French hill station near the Chinese border, Sa Pa offers breathtaking mountain scenery, trekking and close encounters with ethnic minorities. Spend a couple of days visiting nearby villages and soaking up the highland ambience.

DISTANCE: Day 1: 2km (1.5 miles) walking; Day 2: 4km (2.5 miles) walking, 23km (14 miles) driving
TIME: 2 days
START: Day 1: Catholic chapel; Day 2: Cat Cat village
END: Day 1: radio tower; Day 2: Ta Phin village
POINTS TO NOTE: It is now possible to reach Sa Pa via Lao Cai city on the fast, new Lao Cai express highway, but many people still like to take the classic overnight train journey. If you opt for the train route, make sure you book your return train ticket and hotel in advance. Trains can be very full, especially at weekends. Several night trains depart daily from Tran Quy Cap station (behind the main station on Le Duan Street) at 10pm, arriving at Lao Cai station the following morning at 6–7am. Another, more luxurious, option is to stay at the Topas Ecolodge and travel in style in their own private vehicle direct from Hanoi to the door.

The French had the right idea when they made Sa Pa their hill station in the first half of the 20th century. Sa Pa's cool climate at 1,600m (5,249ft) is similar to that of the Alps, a welcome refuge from the stifling humidity and a reminder of home. Located 360km (223 miles) northwest of Hanoi and dramatically perched on the edge of a high plateau, Sa Pa has a stunning location, framed by soaring blue peaks and sweeping valleys dotted with paddy fields and ethnic-minority villages.

Since the French departed, Sa Pa was forgotten for about half a century until foreigners rediscovered it in the 1990s. Now with a huge number of hotels for every budget, the town may have lost a little of its soul, but it is still charming. It is the perfect base to explore the stupendous outlying scenery and ethnic minority villages, where traditional daily life carries on as it has for centuries. And it doesn't get much better than relaxing on a balcony with Mount Fansinpan (Phan Si Pan) – the highest peak in Indochina – looming above. The best times to visit are Sep-

In front of the Catholic chapel

tember to November and March to May. The rainy summer months, particularly July and August, are Sa Pa's busiest months (with the most expensive hotel rates), when Hanoians flock here to escape the heat. Temperatures can plummet in winter, with frost and occasional snow.

After a nine-hour train ride from Hanoi, catch a minivan up the mountain to Sa Pa. Local hotels can organise transfers from Lao Cai, but there are also tourist minibuses which await incoming trains for the 39km (24-mile) drive to Sa Pa. As you zigzag your way uphill from Lao Cai, enjoying spectacular views of the breathtaking Hoang Lien Son mountain range, bear in mind that the French colonialists were carried up here by sedan chair.

AROUND TOWN

After checking into your hotel in the morning and enjoying breakfast, head to the market to gather supplies for a picnic lunch.

Sa Pa Market
Walk up the road to the square with the quaint little **Catholic chapel** ❶ (Nha Tho Sa Pa) and explore the **town market** ❷ from there. You'll encounter lots of Dzao and H'mong ladies selling blankets, silver trinkets, jaw harps and other handicrafts and souvenirs. Keep an eye out for another unique item in the butcher stalls: dog

meat. Unlike other parts of Vietnam, the local vendors will follow you all morning – everywhere you go – until you've made a purchase. Don't bother appeasing them right away; they will just be replaced by others. The best strategy is simply to smile, be patient, and try to make the most of the extra company.

In the recent past, Sa Pa used to be sold on the pretext of a Saturday night 'Love Market', where young minorities coyly met potential suitors in the town centre. This form of voyeuristic tourism, however, has been frowned on, and the tradition has largely moved to a more secluded area.

Walks
In the afternoon consider a hike around the lake and park, northeast of the town square, for scenic views of the modern town. As you pass to the lake you'll pass **The Gecko Restaurant**, see ❶, which makes a good lunch stop. Afterwards, hike up to the **radio tower** ❸, about 300m/yds behind the chapel, for spectacular views of the town and valley below.

Nightlife
Late in the afternoon walk south on Cau May Street to the tourist area, where you'll encounter an array of welcoming Alpine shops, restaurants and bars. Grab dinner at **The Hill Station**, see ❷, further down the road at 7 Muong Hoa Street.

Red Dao women in Ta Phin   *Rice terraces*

H'MONG AND DAO VILLAGES

The main reason to come to Sa Pa is the opportunity to trek through ethnic minority villages and enjoy overnight homestays and hospitality in local stilt houses, especially since government restrictions have been lifted. Several outlying villages – Cat Cat, Ta Van, Sin Chai, Lao Chai and Ta Phin – make pleasant and relatively easy treks. Those in good physical condition can also consider more strenuous treks.

Start the morning of your second day with breakfast at **Sapa Rooms** on Phan Xi Pan Street, see ❸. Ask them to pack a lunch for you, or else pick something up in the Sa Pa market as you walk 3km (2 miles) southwest of town down Phan Si Street to **Cat Cat village**. Cat Cat is a beautiful, traditional Black H'mong village perched on the slopes of a hanging valley. Walk down the steep paths through the village to the river below, and then catch a motorbike back to Sa Pa.

For the afternoon, arrange a motorbike or guided tour to **Ta Phin village**, 10km (6 miles) from Sa Pa back towards Lao Cai, with a marked turnoff. Get dropped off at the start of this traditional Red Dao village, then walk through to the other side and visit the caves on the hill. Children will be eager to guide you into the caves with a torch for a tip.

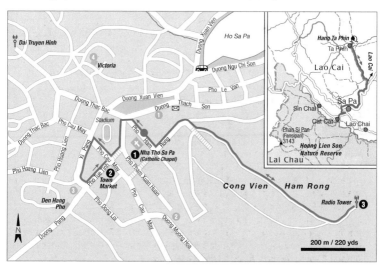

Black H'mong people

Return to Sa Pa for a romantic dinner at **Ta Van** at the Victoria Sapa Hotel, see ❶.

OUTLYING ETHNIC-MINORITY VILLAGES AND MARKETS

As villages close to Sa Pa are becoming increasingly commercialised, many operators are now venturing further afield, hiking to more remote mountain villages and scenery. Try to trek with a local guide, as they understand the local dialects, etiquette and customs better and are able to explain a good deal more besides. Bring good walking boots, insect repellent, water and medical kit.

A number of fascinating but remote weekly ethnic-minority markets – located several hours from Sa Pa – offer a glimpse into much more traditional market life. Can Cau (Saturday), Coc Ly (Tuesday) and Muong Hom (Sunday), all found near the Chinese border, are highly recommended. Colourful, vibrant Bac Ha Market starts early Sunday morning in Bac Ha, roughly 80km (50 miles) east of Sa Pa.

Recommended local tour operators are: Handspan Adventure Travel (8 Cau May Street; tel: 020-387 2110; www.handspan.com) and Topas Adventure Vietnam (21 Muong Hoa Street; tel: 020-387 1331; www.topastravel.vn).

Ethnic minorities

Nearly two-thirds of Vietnam's ethnic-minority groups live in the northern mountainous regions – hence the name *Les montagnards*. Each with their own distinctive dress, customs and dialects, they subsist mostly through farming – rice and maize – cultivated on terraced fields. Sa Pa's main groups are the Giay, Tay, Xa Pho, but predominantly the Black H'mong and Red Dao. The Black H'mong are totally at ease with foreigners, and are recognisable by their indigo-blue hemp attire. Many H'mong females are excellent local guides, speak good English and have savvy sales techniques. On the streets of Sa Pa, they literally mob tourists with their handicraft wares. The Red Dao (pronounced 'Zao') are generally shyer but more striking with their scarlet turban-style headdress, embroidered clothes and often shaved head and eyebrows.

MOUNT FANSIPAN

Looming ominously over Sa Pa, **Mount Fansipan** (Phan Si Pan) entices the more adventurous to conquer its summit, conditions permitting. The mountain stands at 3,143m (10,311ft) in the middle of Hoang Lien Son Nature Reserve, 5km (3 miles) from Sa Pa. Vietnam's highest mountain offers stunning panoramic views.

Silver jewellery for sale   *Mount Fansipan viewed from Sa Pa*

While it is not too technically demanding, climbing Fansipan is still a challenging experience. It is normally tackled over two days up and down the steep, overgrown trails. The time required is very much dependent on weather conditions. If you decide to make the ascent make sure that you arrange the trip with experienced operators that offer two- to four-day packages with all the necessary porters, guides and equipment, like tents and cooking facilities. A controversial cable car is soon to open, providing easy access to the summit for all.

When staying in the area, Topas Ecolodge (tel: 020-387 2404; www. topasecolodge.com) offers highly recommended accommodation outside of Sa Pa itself. It has individual, eco-managed and solar-powered lodges set atop two remote hills, about a 1.5-hour drive from the town. The same company now also operates the Nam Cang Riverside Lodge (www.namcangriversidelodge.com) down in the valley and a stay at both properties makes the ideal mountain escape.

A significant bonus of staying at either of these properties is that you will then trek in areas that are far less heavily touristed than the routes around Sa Pa itself.

Food and drink

① THE GECKO RESTAURANT
Ham Rom Street, near the Post Office; tel: 020-387 1504; daily B, L & D; $$$
The Gecko Restaurant is Sa Pa's first French restaurant and one of the original expat venues. Italian and American favourites also feature on the menu: pizza, hamburgers, pancakes, spaghetti and more. There is also a sister outlet, 'Le Petit Gecko', on Xuan Vien Street.

② THE HILL STATION
7 Muong Hoa; tel: 020 3887 111; www.the hillstation.com; daily B, L & D; $$$
Run by two Norwegians, the Hill Station has plenty of Nordic style. The menu includes excellent burgers and a range of cold cut and cheese platters. The house red is good and the beers are served cold.

③ SAPA ROOMS
18 Phan Xi Pan Street; www.saparooms.com; tel: 020-38722388; daily B, L & D; $$$
Brilliantly decorated with ethnic fabrics and unique furnishings, Sapa Rooms is known for its superb cakes, hearty breakfasts and good coffee.

④ TA VAN
In the Victoria Sapa Hotel; tel: 020-387 1522; www.victoriahotels.asia.com; daily B, L & D; $$$$
Fine dining at its finest with decadent and tasteful surrounds.

Exploring fishing villages by rowboat in Halong Bay

HALONG BAY

Spend two or three days cruising around Halong Bay, one of the most magnificent natural splendours of Asia and a World Heritage Site since 1994. Swathed in legends and beauty and only about three hours from Hanoi, this World Heritage Site should not be missed.

DISTANCE: Dependent on tour operator and length of tour
TIME: 2 or 3 days
START/END: Hanoi
POINTS TO NOTE: Explore Halong Bay by boat. It pays to go on an organised tour. Generally, these offer a package of meals, guide, boat, accommodation and transfers. Boats depart daily from Bai Chay Tourist Wharf in Ha Long City, 165km (102 miles) east of Hanoi by road. The best time to visit is in warmer weather from April to October, as you can swim off the boat. However, during the typhoon season, which peaks in August, boats may cancel trips due to bad weather. All tour operators use engine-powered wooden boats, most with private cabins. Buffalo Tours (tel: 04-3828 0702; www.buffalotours. com) operates some of the best boats and also a seaplane. Handspan Adventure Travel (tel: 04-3926 2828; www.handspan.com) and Topas Travel (www.topastravel.vn) are two other highly regarded agents.

Few could fail to be impressed with Halong Bay, with over 3,000 limestone islands jutting out of emerald-green waters in the Gulf of Bac Bo. In an area covering 1,500 sq km (579 sq miles), sampans, junks, fishing boats – and many tourist boats – sail past a fairytale backdrop of mostly uninhabited limestone karsts, which yield grottoes, secluded coves, coral beaches and hidden lagoons.

The route begins with a three- to four-hour road journey from Hanoi to Ha Long City, where you will board the boat contracted by your tour provider.

Food and drink

① THE GREEN MANGO
Group 19, Block 4, Cat Ba Island; tel: 031 388-7151; www.greenmango.vn; daily B, L & D; $$$$
Cat Ba is very short on good dining options, other than the local style seafood joints, which are rather hit and miss. Green Mango remains the best bet with Western, Vietnamese and fusion cuisine.

Cat Co Beach on Cat Ba Island

ISLANDS AND GROTTOES

Halong Bay looks the stuff of legends. Geologists believe that the karst outcrops were formed by a giant limestone seabed eroding until only pinnacles remained behind. Your boat will visit a couple of the 15 caves open to the public, while en route. Tickets are purchased at the Tourist Wharf or are included in tour packages. The best known is found on the island nearest to Ha Long City: the **Grotto of Wooden Stakes** ❶ (Hang Dau Go), where General Tran Hung Dao amassed hundreds of stakes prior to his 1288 victory. On the same island, the **Grotto of the Heavenly Palace** ❷ (Hang Thien Cung) has some impressive stalactites and stalagmites, as does **Surprise Grotto** ❸ (Hang Sung Sot) on an island further south.

CAT BA ISLAND

After a night on the boat, where you will also eat your meals, spend the following morning enjoying activities on the water. In the afternoon, visit **Cat Ba Island** ❹, the largest in Halong Bay at 354 sq km (136 sq miles), which offers a spectacular, rugged landscape of forested limestone peaks, coral reefs, coastal mangrove and freshwater swamps, lakes and waterfalls. Almost three quarters of the island and its adjacent waters form a national park with diverse flora and fauna. Some boats dock in the fishing harbour, where mini-hotels and basic tourist services are located. Spend a night here if possible and hike to try and see the endemic and endangered Cat Ba langurs (monkeys). Eat dinner at **The Green Mango**, see ❶, and then head back to Hanoi the following morning.

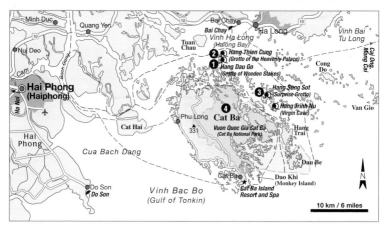

DIRECTORY

Hand-picked hotels and restaurants to suit all budgets and tastes, organised by area, plus select nightlife listings, an alphabetical listing of practical information, a language guide and an overview of the best books and films to give you a flavour of the country.

ACCOMMODATION

Hotel development in the country is flourishing and visitors are spoilt for choice. International chains, with service standards and prices to match, can be found in all the major cities. Luxury hotels and resorts with business centres, wifi, and spas and fitness centres, are all par for the course these days, but there is also plenty of choice in the budget lodgings category, where a room can go for about US$10 a night.

When booking your accommodation, always check the hotel website first for comparison. If it's a smaller outfit without a website, call directly to ask for the best rates. The published rates listed here should only be taken as a guide, as actual prices can be quite elastic – depending on seasonal discounts. Higher-end hotels usually charge a 10 percent tax and 5 percent service charge in addition to the listed prices.

During the school holidays (June–August) the beaches get very crowded, and during the annual Tet festival (in late January or early February) buses and trains are packed with domestic travellers. Hotel rates also spike during the Christmas and New Year periods. If you are making a trip during any of these times, it would be a good idea to book ahead.

> Price for a double room for one night without breakfast:
> $$$$ = over US$100
> $$$ = US$50–100
> $$ = US$20–50
> $ = below US$20

Central Highlands

Bao Dai Villa
Lak Lake; tel: 0500-358 6184; www.daklak tourist.com.vn; $
Now rather tired, this old house is located on grounds that were used as a holiday home by the last emperor. It includes six rooms which are large, but in need of a makeover. If available, try for the massive King's Room, which is adorned with his own portraits. The restaurant features striking black and white photos of the emperor and his elephants.

Damsan Hotel
212–214 Nguyen Cong Tru Street, Buon Ma Thuot; tel: 0500-385 1234; www.damsan hotel.com.vn; $
Damsan is one of the nicest hotels in town, with a pool, tennis court and large restaurant, but it is now quite dated. Service is good and so is the staff's English level; and rooms are comfortable. A coffee shop and bar with balconies is located across the street at Da Quy.

Indochine Hotel
30 Bach Dang Street, Kontum; tel: 060-386 3335; www.indochinehotel.vn; $

View over Da Lat

Indochine (aka Dong Duong Indochine) is perhaps the best hotel in town. The views of the Dak Bla River and mountains from Indochine are fantastic, the rooms spacious and comfortable. A riverfront pool makes a great place for evening drinks and watching the sunset. Free breakfast is included.

Da Lat

Da Lat Palace
12 Tran Phu Street, Da Lat; tel: 063-382 5444; www.dalatresorts.com/index.php/en/dalatpalace; $$$$

Da Lat's original luxury hotel (previously managed by Sofitel) is the best choice if you want to be transported back into the time of the French colonials. The hotel originally opened in 1922, and although it was completely renovated in 1995, it is still dripping in old-world charm and elegance. Rooms are furnished in period French style and have fireplaces.

Dreams Hotel
151 Phan Dinh Phung; tel: 063-383 3748; www.dreamshoteldalat.com; $

Run by an extremely welcoming and friendly family, Dreams is a great budget pick. The price includes a large breakfast with seriously strong Vietnamese coffee.

Evason Ana Mandara Villas Da Lat
Le Loi Street, Da Lat; tel: 063-355 5888; www.anamandara-resort.com; $$$$

This is the most luxurious resort in Da Lat, secluded on the southwest side of town. The resort has a rustic elegance with 17 restored French colonial villas dating from the 1920s and 1930s. Service and pampering are the focal points, with private butlers assigned to every room.

Da Nang

Furama Resort Da Nang
68 Ho Xuan Huong Street; My An Beach; tel: 0511-384 7888; www.furamavietnam.com; $$$$

Furama was the first 5 star to arrive in Da Nang and it remains one of the best despite its age. The spacious rooms are surrounded by landscaped gardens, and there are two swimming pools and a golf driving range. Furama has a fully equipped fitness centre and several excellent, albeit expensive, restaurants.

Fusion Maia Resort
Son Tra – Dien Ngoc Coastal Street, My Khe Ward; tel: 0511-396 7999; www.fusion-resorts.com; $$$$

The Fusion resorts offer a one-of-a-kind luxury experience with unlimited spa treatments included in the price. Each room comes with its own private pool, sunken black granite bathtub, fully loaded iPod and free WiFi. The king-sized four-poster beds with swivel widescreen TV (also viewable from the tub) are enough to keep you in the room all day.

Fusion Suites
Vo Nguyen Giap; tel 0511-3991 9777; www.fusionsuitesdanangbeach.com

A room at the Hilton Hanoi Opera

On the beachfront with a pool right by the sand, Fusion Suites offers modern rooms and large, apartment-like suites complete with kitchens. Many rooms have amazing views of the beach and Son Tra Peninsula.

Orange Hotel

29 Hoang Dieu; tel: 0511 3566 176; http://danangorangehotel.com; $$$
With fantastic staff, this economical 3 star hotel is good value for money in a downtown location. Surrounded by a wealth of good food options (including Com Ga A Hai around the corner) and plenty of cafés.

Ha Long Bay

Catba Island Resort and Spa

Cat Co 1 Beach, Cat Ba Island; tel: 031-368 8686; www.catbaislandresort-spa.com; $$$
Set on a hill and surrounded by forest, this plush resort features tastefully outfitted rooms with gorgeous views of the bay and Cat Co Beach. There is also a great free-form pool with waterslides and private beach to lounge away the day. The on-site restaurant serves Asian, Western and seafood dishes.

Hanoi

6 on Sixteen

16 Bao Khanh; tel: 04-6673 6729; http://6-on-sixteen-boutique.hanoihotelsvietnam.net; $$$
Six thoughtfully decorated rooms from the man behind Tet Decor, Pete Wilkes. In his signature style, there are plenty of ethnic minority fabric touches and unique pieces of furniture.

Church Hotel

9 Nha Tho Street, Hoan Kiem District; tel: 04-3928 8118; www.churchhotel.com.vn; $$
This gem of a boutique hotel, steps away from St Joseph's Cathedral, was built in 2004 and features stylish rooms overlooking trendy Nha Tho Street and the Ba Da Pagoda. Try to get a room facing the back, where it's quieter. All rooms include free wifi and breakfast.

Golden Lotus

29 Hang Trong; tel: 0439380900; www.goldenlotushotel.com.vn; $$
In a central location on the edge of the Old Quarter and a short walk to Hoan Kiem lake, the Golden Lotus has a wide range of tastefully appointed rooms and suites with dark woods, crisp white linens and old black and white photographs of old Hanoi.

Hanoi Elegance Hotel II

85 Ma May Street, Hoan Kiem District; tel: 04-3926 3451; www.elegancehospitality.com; $$
Hanoi Elegance is a modern hotel built in 2006, right in the heart of the Old Quarter. The rooms are large, airy and well furnished; friendly, helpful staff speak good English and are eager to please. The hotel can arrange tours to many of the outlying attractions.

The pool at the Sofitel Plaza Hanoi

Hilton Hanoi Opera

1 Le Thanh Tong Street, Hoan Kiem District; tel: 04-3933 0500; www.hanoi.hilton.com; $$$$

The Hilton is an architecturally impressive hotel, built to complement the neighbouring Opera House. Rooms are large, airy and modern, and the Vietnamese-style rooms are a particular treat. The wide, spacious lobby features live music and free WiFi. The hotel also has a great pool, gym and spa.

Hanoi Paradise Hotel

53 Hang Chieu Street; tel: 04-3929 0026; www.hanoiparadisehotel.com; $$$

One of few Old Quarter hotels to boast a pool, this spotlessly clean hotel features large, well-kept rooms and very helpful staff. Opened in 2006, all rooms have an internet-connected computer. Free bottle of red wine, fruit and flowers on arrival.

Intercontinental Westlake Hanoi

1A Nghi Tam Street; tel: 04-6270 8888; www.hanoi.intercontinental.com; $$$$

The Intercontinental is a luxurious hotel, built over a picturesque part of West Lake. The rooms are large, comfortable and elegantly outfitted, and the hotel pool and gym are unmatched in Hanoi. Staff are helpful, if restrained. Features three restaurants and two bars. Watching the sunset at the Sunset Bar is a must.

Joseph's Hotel

5 Au Trieu; 091-309 0446; www.josephs hotel.com; $$

On a sliver of a road down the side of St Joseph's Cathedral, this friendly hotel has a range of very comfortable, good value rooms. Choose one at the front of the hotel if you are a light sleeper as the church bells can be heard loud and clear at the rear.

Sofitel Legend Metropole Hanoi

15 Ngo Quyen Street, Hoan Kiem District; tel: 04-3826 6919; www.sofitel.com; $$$$

Built in 1901 and renovated by the French Sofitel company in 2005, this grande dame has maintained its colonial-era atmosphere while improving on its comfort levels. Former guests include kings, princes, presidents and an assortment of celebrities. Rooms in both the original Metropole Wing and newer Opera Wing are beautifully appointed, but the latter has larger and more contemporary-style rooms.

Sofitel Plaza Hanoi

1 Thanh Nien St; tel: 04-3823 8888; www.sofitel.com/Hanoi; $$$$

The 20-storey Sofitel Plaza dominates the skyline at the edge of West Lake and is home to the best indoor/outdoor swimming pool in the city. The hotel has quiet, stylish rooms, two restaurants and a spa. The sunset views from the Summit Lounge are not to be missed.

Ho Chi Minh City

Caravelle Hotel

19 Lam Son Square, District 1; tel: 08-3823 4999; www.caravellehotel.com; $$$$

Famous Caravelle Hotel

Opened 1959, the 5-star Caravelle is one of the city's most celebrated international hotels, yet it is not part of a generic chain. A glitzy 24-floor edifice, the original low-rise wing was famously home to foreign press corps during the Vietnam War. Past guests have included dignitaries, politicians and celebrities, plus it's a corporate favourite.

Elios

233 Pham Ngu Lao Street, District 1; tel: 08-3838 5585; www.elioshotel.vn; $$
Located in the heart of the backpacker district, this favourite new 3-star hotel has slightly higher standards than others in this price category. The rooms are bright, comfortable and modestly sized; superior rooms are a bit larger. The rooftop restaurant-bar offers good views and is a great place to unwind. Elios also has a gym, meeting rooms and lift.

Lan Lan Hotel

246 Thu Khoa Huan; tel: 08-3822 7926; www.lanlanhotel.com.vn; $$
Very good value for money hotel with large rooms, excellent service and a buffet breakfast included. Great central location and superb views from the rooms on the upper floors.

Lavender Central Hotel

208–210 Le Thanh Ton Street, District 1; tel: 08-2222 8888; www.lavenderhotel.com.vn; $$$
The Lavender Hotel is a firm favourite for its stylish, intimate ambience and great

pricing. Located behind Ben Thanh Market, all rooms are nicely decorated and feature rain showers in the bathrooms and flat-screen TVs (note some rooms don't have windows, so ask to check).

Park Hyatt Saigon

2 Lam Son Square; tel: 08-3824 1234; www.saigon.park.hyatt.com; $$$$
The elegant Hyatt evokes a nostalgic feel from the city's French Indochina era, while offering all manner of modern facilities. With a vantage point overlooking the Municipal Theatre, it oozes class and luxury. The rooms feature colonial touches like four-poster beds and modern amenities like rain showers and huge flat-screen TVs.

Renaissance Riverside Hotel Saigon

8-15 Ton Duc Thang Street; tel: 08-3822 0033; www.renaissancehotels.com/sgnbr; $$$$
Located downtown along the river, this 5-star offers high standards with a boutique-style vibe and exceptional service. Most of the rooms and suites are on the small side, but offer superb river views and luxurious bedding. Highlights include the 22nd-floor rooftop terrace pool, elegant 5th-floor Atrium Lounge and Chinese restaurant.

Hoi An

Anantara Hoi An Resort

1 Pham Hong Thai Street; tel: 0510-391 4555; www.hoi-an.anantara.com; $$$$

A river view suite at the Anantara Hoi An Resort

Located on the banks of the Thu Bon River just next to the Old Town, this is one of Hoi An's top resorts. An exceptional buffet breakfast is served in the upper level restaurant with river views; the spa offers excellent treatments including massage; and a range of tours can be booked.

The Nam Hai

Hamlet 1, Hoi An; tel: 0510-394 0000; www.ghmhotels.com/en/nam-hai; $$$$

Stratospheric prices aside, this is easily Vietnam's most exclusive beach resort (and probably one of its most expensive). The smallest room is an oversized 80 sq metres villa while the one-bedroom villas with their own private pools are a mere 250 sq metres. Includes three stunning infinity-edged swimming pools and an exquisite spa; and served possibly the best buffet and a la carte breakfast in the land.

Palm Garden Resort

Lac Long Quan, Cua Dai Beach; tel: 0510-392 7927; www.palmgardenresort.com.vn; $$$$

A secluded resort set in mature, lush gardens on a private stretch of beach, just 5 minutes' drive from Hoi An. Facilities include a fitness centre and four eating and drinking options. There are plenty of water-sports activities available at the beach, including windsurfing, sea kayaking, sailing, jet-skiing and parasailing

Villa Hoa Su

5, Cam Thanh Ward; tel: 05103933933; www.villahoasu.com; $$$

Just outside the main town, Villa Hoa Su is a true haven with just a handful of exceptional rooms arranged around a peaceful central pool with the scent of frangipani trees filling the air.

Hue

Hotel Saigon Morin

30 Le Loi Street; tel: 054-382 3526; www.morinhotel.com.vn; $$$

This historical legend first opened in 1901 and retains much of its old French colonial charm. Conveniently located across the street from the Perfume River, it's within walking distance of the Dong Ba Market and Royal Citadel. The garden courtyard restaurant serves international cuisine, with a live orchestra playing traditional Vietnamese court music every evening.

La Residence Hotel & Spa

5 Le Loi Street; tel: 054-383 7475; www.la-residence-hue.com; $$$$

Now part of the M Gallery chain, this hotel occupies the former home of the French governor. The lovely rooms have Art Deco furnishings, four-poster beds and terraces overlooking the Perfume River and the flagstaff of the Royal Citadel. A spa and fine-dining options are on-site.

Ngoc Binh Hotel

6/34 Nguyen Tri Phuong Street; tel: 054-381 9860; www.ngocbinhhotel.com; $

Enjoy the view at Evason Ana Mandara

Conveniently located in the centre of town, the staff are helpful and friendly, and the facilities are disabled-friendly (with a lift system). There is free pick-up from the train and bus stations. Rooms have everything a backpacker could want, including satellite TV, A/C, telephones and hot water.

Mekong Delta

Cuu Long Hotel

1 Road 15, Vinh Long; tel: 070-382 3616; www.cuulongtourist.com; $

There is not a big range of choices for accommodation in Vinh Long, but Cuu Long is the best. It comprises two blocks: A and B. The latter is newer and has more modern facilities. All rooms are spacious and comfortable with en suite bathrooms, and command scenic views over the river.

Victoria Can Tho

Cai Khe Ward, Can Tho; tel: 071-381 0111; www.victoriahotels-asia.com; $$$

This elegant colonial-style resort lies on the banks of the Hau River. Located close to town, but tucked away from the action, all its well-appointed rooms feature furnishings that blend traditional handicrafts with colonial-style design. Balconies look out over the river, pool or gardens.

Nha Trang

Evason Ana Mandara

Tran Phu Street; tel: 058-352 2222; www.sixsenses.com; $$$$

Part of the luxury Six Senses resort chain, the Ana Mandara occupies a slice of urban beach. This elegant property has two swimming pools, two restaurants and two bars, a water sports centre and PADI scuba-diving facility. The villas are beautifully furnished and well appointed.

Mia Resort Nha Trang

Bai Dong, Cam Hai Dong, Cam Lam; tel: 058-3989 666; www.mianhatrang.com $$$$

This extremely luxurious and secluded resort is located just south of the city on the way to Cam Ranh Bay. The signature Sandals Restaurant serves seafood, Asian fusion and imaginative pizzas.

Sao Mai Hotel

99 Nguyen Thien Thuat Street; tel: 058-352 6412; www.sao-mai.nha-trang-hotels.net; $

This friendly, family-run hotel is one of the best-value digs in town. The large, tidy rooms have fan or A/C, hot water, fridge and TV.

Around Mui Ne

Ho Phong Hotel

363 Ngo Gia Tu Street, Phan Rang; tel: 068-392 0333; email: hophong@yahoo.com; $

Just off the main drag on the south side of town, Ho Phong is a great value hotel, with clean and spacious rooms. Rooms have A/C or fans and satellite TV. Complimentary internet access is provided. Minimal English is spoken, but the staff

The Victoria Can Tho

are friendly and do their best to meet your needs.

Mia Resort Mui Ne (Sailing Club)
24 Nguyen Dinh Chieu Street, Mui Ne; tel: 062-384 7440; www.miamuine.com; $$$$
Mia Resort is part of the renowned Sailing Club chain and a favourite of expats and water sports enthusiasts. Mia offers private bungalows hidden among tropical gardens with a beachside pool and bar. Xanh Spa, Sandals Restaurant and Storm Kiteboarding are all located on site.

Mui Ne Backpackers
137 Nguyen Dinh Chieu, Mui Ne; tel: 062-384 7047; www.muinebackpackers.com; $
Previously known as Nha Tro Kim Hong, Mui Ne Backpackers is one of the oldest local accommodations, and remains a backpacker favourite to this day. Dorms, private rooms and beachside bungalows are all on offer, with a swimming pool out front.

Victoria Phan Thiet Beach Resort & Spa
Km 9, Phu Hai St; tel: 062-381 3000; www.victoriahotels-asia.com; $$$$
A landmark in Mui Ne, this property has a long-standing reputation for quality and service. The resort is set on its own private stretch of beach just outside the main drag of resorts and restaurants, which means it's always peaceful. Facilities include horse riding, fitness centre, spa, two swimming pools, Wi-Fi access and childcare services.

Chau Long Sapa Hotel
24 Dong Loi St; tel: 020-387 1245; www.chaulonghotel.com; $$
Large, elegantly designed rooms come complete with stunning views over the valley. The friendly and knowledgeable staff are a great source of information. Also features a spa, plus a large buffet breakfast is included.

Topas Eco Lodge
24 Muong Hoa St; tel: 020-387 1331; www.topasecolodge.com; $$$$
Located 20km (12.4 miles) south of Sa Pa, the Ecolodge has one of the most beautiful settings imaginable, with individual bungalows clustered around a hilltop overlooking commanding views of the mountains and valleys. Actively farmed rice terraces stretch right up to the restaurant's terrace, meaning guests can watch rice cultivation as it happens. The lodge also runs great tours to the less touristed parts of the region.

Victoria Sapa Resort
Sa Pa Town; tel: 020-387 1522; www.victoriahotels-asia.com; $$$$
This charming chalet-style resort is located just above the town, and offers stunning views of the valley and Mount Fansipan. Rooms are warm and luxurious with unique Vietnamese accents. The property features a beautiful pool, garden and spa. The resort can arrange its own train transfers on board the exclusive Victoria Express from Hanoi.

ACCOMMODATION **109**

Hanoi's dining scene extends from smart restaurants...

RESTAURANTS

Vietnam has seen an explosion of new restaurants in recent years, with Hanoi and Ho Chi Minh City now home to restaurants offering almost any cuisine you can think of. Hoi An, too, now has a healthy choice of international food options alongside the excellent Vietnamese menus on available.

However, for many people, it is the street food and no-nonsense hole-in-the-wall style eateries that make Vietnam such a wonderful culinary destination. From the *bun cha* in Hanoi to the *my quang* of Hoi An and on to the seafood of Nha Trang and the endless variety of Saigon street kitchens, Vietnam is the culinary nation that keeps on giving and which a foodie could hungrily explore for a lifetime.

The restaurant guide gives an overview of the country's restaurants rather than street food kitchens, for which it is simply often best to follow your nose and head where the locals are eating.

Note that Vietnamese do not have the same definition of vegetarian that is understood in the West. 'Vegetarian' dishes may still contain pork fat or fish sauce. The best places to find vegetarian food are in stalls outside active pagodas.

Peanuts are a common ingredient in Vietnamese cuisine, particularly in dipping sauces. If you do not want peanuts in your food (for example, if you have a peanut allergy), you may request 'Lam on khong cho toi dau phong' (Please don't give me peanuts).

Anything that is placed on the table but not ordered will usually appear on the bill as an additional charge. The only exceptions are usually ice tea (but not always), and bread at Italian or upscale restaurants. Better restaurants may charge an additional 10 percent tax and 5 percent service charge to the bill as well.

> Cost of a meal for one including up to three dishes and a drink:
> $$$$ = over US$15
> $$$ = US$10–15
> $$ = US$5–10
> $ = under US$5

Da Lat

Dalat Train Cafe
1 Quang Trung; tel: 063-381 6365; www.dalattrainvilla.com; $
The quirkiest of the city's eateries and housed inside a train carriage, this is a quaint spot for a cheap bite to eat. Expect a range of western dishes with an American diner touch and some good cocktails to round out your meal.

Le Rabelais
12 Tran Phu Street; tel: 063-382 5444; $$$$

Ambience is the draw here in this French-style dining room with its views of the lake. Service is the best in town and the French food is well executed. A smart dress code is strictly enforced, so dress your best and step back in time for an evening.

V Cafe

1 Bui Thi Xuan Street; tel: 063-352 02153; www.vcafedalatvietnam.com; $$$

Run by an American-Vietnamese partnership, V Cafe serves winter warmers and comfort food alongside a small range of Vietnamese dishes. Live music every night makes this the most fun place for dinner. Especially warm and welcoming on a cold evening.

Da Nang

Apsara Restaurant

222 Tran Phu Street; tel: 0511-356 1409; $$$

This upscale restaurant near the Cham museum serves fresh seafood and local delicacies with a Cham theme. You'll pass a recreated Cham tower in miniature (although it still looms high above) as you enter. Nightly traditional Cham music and dance shows are scheduled from 6.30–8pm.

Com Ga A Hai

100 Thai Phien; tel: 0511-390 6908; $$

So popular it now spreads across two locations on opposite sides of the road, A Hai's *com ga* (chicken rice) is legendary. The grilled chicken here has a

unique taste and comes with perfectly cooked rice and a small side salad.

Fat Fish

439 Tran Hung Dao; tel: 0511-3944 5707; www.fatfishdanang.com; $$

From Duc Tran, the man behind Hoi An's Mango Mango and Mango Rooms, Fat Fish serves international cuisine in a modern setting with Pasteur Street craft ales on tap. Good pizzas and fish dishes.

The Waterfront

150 Bach Dang Street; tel: 09 2507 5580; www.waterfrontdanang.com; $$$–$$$$

This modern resto-bar on the riverfront on Danang's main road features a restaurant area upstairs, comfortable bar seating downstairs and floor to ceiling windows for views across the water. The menu includes great grills and burgers and a range of seafood options. The well stocked bar features good beer and wines.

Hanoi

Bun Cha Huong Lien

24 Le Van Huu Street; tel: 096-696 2683: $

Every lunch time Hanoi is filled with the tantalising aroma of BBQ pork as the capital's lunch staple, *bun cha*, is prepared. There are probably hundreds of excellent *bun cha* options in Hanoi, but this one on Le Van Huu Street is worth seeking out not only for the main course, but also for their unique take on seafood spring rolls.

Opulent decor at a café in HCMC

Chim Sao

65 Ngo Hue Street; tel: 04-3976 0633;
www.chimsao.com; $$–$$$$

Fantastic Vietnamese food in a laid back atmosphere. Sit on the floor upstairs and enjoy the art hanging on the walls or opt for table and chairs dining on the ground floor. Don't miss the sautéed duck and the frog. Also features excellent northern sticky rice and good spring rolls. The apple rice wine is the most palatable we've tried.

Hanoi Social Club

6 Hoi Vu, tel: 04-3938 2117; $$

On pretty Hoi Vu street, this beautifully restored town house has funky decor and furnishings, consistently good tunes on the stereo and well made coffee, including flat whites. Excellent pulled pork sandwiches and a wide range of choices for veggies. Also plays host to plenty of live music events.

Highway 4 Bar & Restaurant

5 Hang Tre Street; tel: 04-3926 0639; 54 Mai Hac De Street; tel: 04-3976 2647; $$$

Highway 4 specialises in exotic rice wine liquors and North Vietnamese cuisine, especially hotpot, fish, spring rolls (try the catfish spring rolls with wasabi-based dip) and carmelised clay pot dishes. Amid traditional northern decor, sit cross-legged at low split-bamboo tables or opt for more conventional seating if you prefer.

Maison de Tet Decor

36 Duong Ven Ho; tel: 096 661 1383,
www.tet-lifestyle-collection.com; $$

Housed in a grand villa on the shores of West Lake, Tet Decor is a wonderfully homely cafe-cum-restaurant serving a range of healthy food, excellent cakes and very good coffee. Beautifully furnished by owner Pete Wilkes, this is a great place to unwind for a few hours.

Mau Dich 37

37 Nam Trang; tel: 04-3715 4336; $$

Harking back to a bygone era of rationing, Mau Dich serves old school Hanoi staples in a very cool, retro themed space. Be sure to get a seat in the front room.

Net Hue

36C Mai Hac DeStreet; tel: 04-3944 9769;
$–$$

The decor is not the draw at this no-nonsense eatery where tables are rammed in and the turnover is rapid. The focus here, as the name suggests, is Hue food, and it is actually better than most places in the city itself. Order as much as you can and don't miss the che desserts – try the banana version.

Pho Bat Dan

49 Bat Dan Street; $

One of the longest running, no-nonsense *pho* (noodle soup) joints in the capital and still one of the best. Service certainly

does not often come with a smile, but that's not what people come here for.

Pho Cuon Hung Ben

26 Nguyen Khac Hieu; tel: 0438 292 040; $

One of many similar places in the Truc Bach area, Hung Ben is opposite a beautiful temple and serves excellent *pho cuon* – ground beef and herbs wrapped in sheets of rice noodle. Try the *pho chien phong* too.

Pots n Pans

57 Bui Thi Xuan Street; tel: 04-3944 0204; $$$$

Managed by graduates of the KOTO training school, Pots n Pans is an upmarket fusion restaurant set in chic surrounds with excellent service and unique cuisine. The downstairs bar mixes excellent cocktails.

Quan An Ngon

18 Phan Boi Chau Street; tel: 04-3942 8162; $$$

This successful HCMC venture has found equal success in Hanoi. Sit at simple tables set in a pretty alfresco villa courtyard and enjoy traditional Vietnamese dishes served from the surrounding mock street food stalls. The restaurant can get very busy, but is open all day.

Ray Quan

8A Nguyen Khuyen; tel: 09-1357 8588; $$

Set on the train tracks that cut right through the heart of Hanoi within inches of front doors, Ray Quan serves up traditional Vietnamese food in a friendly and sometimes lively atmosphere thanks to the extensive rice wine list that the owners will be happy for you to try before you buy.

Ho Chi Minh City

Au Parc

23 Han Thuyen Street; tel: 08-3829 2772; $$–$$$

Greek and Turkish options are the order of the day in this bright cafe space with views of the gardens. The Sunday brunch is particularly good and goes down well with a Bloody Mary.

Ben Thanh Night Market

Phan Boi Chau and Phan Chu Trinh streets, District 1; $–$$$

Post-dusk, open-air, makeshift eateries assemble outside Ben Thanh Market, which serve a huge selection of good-value Vietnamese fare. The streets are packed nightly with locals and tourists in this spot that is ideal for sampling local street food. Dishes include noodle soups, seafood crêpes, fruit salads and shakes, and plenty of seafood. During daylight hours, head inside, where around 25–30 stalls sell a wide range of Vietnamese dishes.

Guc Cach

10 Dang Tat, tel: 08-4801 4410; $$

Designed and run by a famous architect, Guc Cach boasts plenty of character with retro Saigon furnishings and

A typical Hoi An dish

knick knacks. The food is well-cooked, home-style Vietnamese fare.

KOTO Saigon

151A Hai Ba Trung Street; tel: 08-3934 9151; www.koto.com.au; $$–$$$

This is the Saigon version of Hanoi's successful Know One, Teach One (KOTO) restaurant and also operates as a training workplace for disadvantaged youth. As well as some interesting fusion dishes, KOTO serves some Vietnamese dishes with a twist. The new bar is a great place for an evening drink.

Pizza 4Ps

8/15 Le Thanh Ton; tel: 0127894444; www.pizza4ps.com; $$$

With specially made cheeses and organic vegetables sourced from Dalat, the pizzas that come out of the 4P's woodfired kilns are seriously good. Cool decor and swift service.

Quan Ut Ut

168 Vo Van Kiet; tel: 0839144500; www.quanutut.com; $$$

A temple to all things meat, Quan Ut Ut has quickly become a favourite among Saigon's carnivores. Try the mixed platter including ribs and chicken and add on a side of macaroni cheese. The owners also serve their very own craft beer, which hits the spot very nicely on a hot Ho Chi Minh City day.

The Refinery

74 Hai Ba Trung Street, District 1; tel: 08-3823 0509; $$$$

This period French-style bistro is housed in a restored opium refinery, set off the street, behind the Opera House. The menu features a selection of contemporary European dishes and includes home-made ice creams, as well as excellent weekend brunches. Unsurprisingly, the Refinery is a favourite evening hideaway for expats.

Hoi An

Ba Buoi

22 Phan Chu Trinh; tel: 051-086 1151; $

A Hoi An institution, Ba Buoi is a tiny eatery bursting with charm. Quite possibly the best chicken rice in town.

Bale Well

45/11 Tran Hung Dao; $$

Named after the well from which the water used to prepare a truly authentic dish of *cau lau* (a Hoi An staple) is drawn, Bale Well is a long-standing favourite. Excellent *banh xeo* (crispy filled pancakes) and roll-your-own treats. Hidden down an alley off Tran Hung Dao Street.

Good Morning Vietnam

34 Le Loi Street; tel: 0510-391 0227; www.goodmorningviet.com; $$$

Despite having perhaps the worst name of any restaurant in the country, Good Morning Vietnam is one of the best Italians you'll find in Southeast Asia, with particularly excellent pizza as well as quality pastas.

Tacos in HCMC

Hola Taco!
5 Phan Chau Trinh, tel: 091-296 1169; $$
The menu is short here, but the few dishes on offer are executed very well. Great enchiladas and tacos and regular BBQ nights.

Mango Rooms
111 Nguyen Thai Hoc Street; tel: 0510-391 0839; www.mangorooms.com; $$
A bright and breezy place that serves an inventive Vietnamese menu. The Vietnamese chef grew up in the US and gives a decidedly Californian spin to the dishes.

The Market
3 Nguyen Hoang Street; tel: 051-0392 6926; www.msvy-tastevietnam.com; $$$$
Run by the famous Ms Vy, whose Hoi An empire now includes her own boutique hotel and several restaurants, the Market serves a huge range of expertly prepared Vietnamese classics. The salads are superb, the whole red snapper is a delight and the mixed berry smoothie is not to be missed.

Soul Kitchen
An Bang Beach; tel: 096-440 320; www.soulkitchen.sitew.com/#Soul.A; $$$
A 10 minute taxi or pleasant cycle ride from Hoi An out on An Bang Beach, Soul Kitchen is a very easy place to lose a day. Choose from a sun lounger on the beach, a day bed on the lawn or a shaded table. The food isn't the main attraction here, but the grilled fish is always a winner. Good tunes on the stereo and live bands on Sunday nights.

Streets Restaurant Café
17 Le Loi Street, 0510-391 1948, www.streetsinternational.org: $$
Part of the Streets International social enterprise group, Streets is a training restaurant for people from disadvantaged backgrounds. Not only is it a feel-good place to eat, the food is first rate too, with Vietnamese and international options on the menu.

Hue

Les Jardins de la Carambole
34 Dang Tran Con Street; tel: 054-3 3 54 88 15; www.lesjardinsdelacarambole.com; $$$$
Set in an old colonial villa, Les Jardins is an offshoot of the long popular Carambole in the heart of town. This is the more intimate and romantic of the two options, with a well thought out menu of French and Vietnamese dishes.

Ganesh
34 Nguyen Tri Phuong Street; tel: 054-382 1616; $$$
The horrendous decor at Ganesh tells you that the food must be excellent, because it is always busy and people are oblivious to the peach and pink walls and ceilings as they devour excellent tandoori and curry, which are consistently excellent, while the naan is unbeatable.

Hang Me Me
16 Vo Thi Sau; tel 054-384 8402;
$
Not a place to come for the decor, Me Me is all about the food with all the Hue specialities on offer. Best visited in a group so you can order a range of dishes and share.

Phuong Nam Café
38 Tran Cao Van Street; tel: 054-384 9317;
$
Despite lots of foreign customers, prices have remained normal and the menu entirely Vietnamese, except for the many pancakes. Service is slow but friendly. Try the *bun thit nuong* (grilled meat and noodles) or the many Hue specialities. This is a long standing Hue institution.

Nha Trang

Da Fernando
96 Nguyen Thien Thuat Street; tel: 058-322 9102; $$$
Fernando formerly helmed Good Morning Vietnam in Mui Ne, but has come into his own in Nha Trang. The menu includes popular favourites – pizza, pasta, gnocchi and risotto – but moves beyond the basics for delightful surprises. Anchovies, sun-dried tomatoes and highly refined olive oil are signature speciality ingredients.

La Mancha
78 Nguyen Thien Thuat Street; tel: 091-456 9782; $$$

La Mancha has the most attentive and cheerful service of any restaurant in the tourist district. This excellent tapas restaurant has a great atmosphere, lively Spanish music and a fountain at the centre. Free fresh bread keeps coming throughout the meal. Try the stewed Spanish sausages.

Omar's
98B Nguyen Thien Thuat Street; tel: 058-322 1615; $$$
Master chef Omar from New Delhi serves a superb mix of meat and vegetarian curries, tandoori barbecues, Indian breads and rice.

Nha Hang Yen
3/2A Tran Quang Khai Street, tel: 093-376 6205
This is packed out every night, so it is best to book ahead or be happy to queue for a while. A good place to try a wide range of very well-executed Vietnamese dishes, with excellent service from staff who will happily talk you through the menu and make suggestions.

Truc Linh 1
11 Biet Thu; tel: 058-352 6742; $$
The Truc Linh eateries are popular seafood venues, where the catch of the day is displayed in enormous tanks on the street. These large, lively restaurants are busy into the night and also serve a wide range of backpacker favourites for non-seafood lovers.

Hue cuisine

Mui Ne

Champa Restaurant

Coco Beach Resort, 58 Nguyen Dinh Chieu; tel: 062-3847 111; $$$

Champa has some of the finest food in Mui Ne, serving French 'cuisine bourgeois'. The restaurant is decorated with Cham art and the large terrace overlooks the gardens and pool. The bar serves Cuban cigars and great cocktails, accompanied by classy French tunes.

Good Morning Vietnam

57 Nguyen Dinh Chieu, Mui Ne; tel: 062-384 7585; www.goodmorningviet.com; $$$

Italian-owned and managed, this Vietnam restaurant chain is a favourite of expats and travellers alike. Pizzas are their claim to fame and justifiably so, although the Hoi An location has the edge on this spot.

Ganesh

57 Nguyen Dinh Chieu Street, Mui Ne; tel: 062-374 1330; $$$

This popular venue serves North Indian and tandoori cuisine to the sounds of lively Indian music. Both the meat and the vegetarian options are excellent.

Jibes Beach Club

Nguyen Dinh Chieu Street; tel: 062-3847405; $$–$$$

Owned by the friendly Pascal who was one of the first people to kick off kite-surfing in town, Jibe's is a chilled out beach bar by day selling beers and burgers. In the evening white table cloths come out making this a very pleasant spot for a glass of wine with sand between your toes.

Vietnam Home

125A, B Nguyen Dinh Chieu, tel: 062-384 7687; $

Set in an atmospheric bamboo treehouse of sorts, Vietnam Home offers a varied menu of local favourites and regional specialties. The food is top-notch at reasonable prices. Occasionally there is a live band; either ethnic Cham or highlands music.

Sa Pa

Sapa Moment Restaurant

033 Muong Hoa, Sa Pa; tel: 090-910 7111; $$$

Small and cosy place serving great Vietnamese and international food. The seafood hot pot is highly recommended.

Ta Van Restaurant

Victoria Sapa Resort, Sa Pa Town; tel: 020-387 1522; www.victoriahotels-asia.com; $$$$

Dine inside the lodge by the fireplace or outside on the terrace with views of Mount Fansipan. The menus include European and Asian favourites, with emphasis on Vietnamese and Cambodian cuisine (the latter is strangely uncommon in Vietnam). Live ethnic music and dance is performed in the evenings.

HCMC at night

NIGHTLIFE

Vietnam's nightlife scene has vastly improved over the last few years, though recent visitors to neighbouring Bangkok or Singapore may find themselves underwhelmed. The most activity is located in HCMC and Hanoi, with a burgeoning scene in Nha Trang and Mui Ne. Vietnam's 'culture police' (no joke, they do exist) have laid off lately, allowing venues to stay open later (larger clubs tend to close at midnight, but smaller venues are open later, and a rare few stay open all night).

Nightlife in Vietnam is generally a very safe experience but precautions necessary in other countries should also be observed here. Don't accept opened drinks from strangers. Women should be careful leaving bars late at night with male moto taxi drivers. Be careful of valuables. Snatch-and-drive thieves often wait for patrons exiting bars.

Hanoi

Culture

Cheo Hanoi Theatre

15 Nguyen Dinh Chieu Street, Hai Ba Trung District; tel: 04-3943 7361

Cheo theatre is a uniquely northern Vietnamese folk art that originated in the Red River Delta. The shows – which incorporate dance, music and drama – depict the ordinary struggles and successes of rural Vietnamese, and often without English translation.

Opera House

1 Trang Tien Street; Hoan Kiem District; tel: 04-3993 0113; www.ticketvn.com

Built in the early 1900s by the French, Hanoi's Opera House holds regular performances of classical and traditional music, as well as dance, by local and foreign artists of note. The performance space is quite small, making for an intimate evening.

Bars

+84

23 Ngo Van So; tel: 09 4876723

From the same people behind Barbetta, +84 is a dimly lit venue with dark red walls, wooden furnishings and regular live music including blues and jazz. Burgers and pastas feature on the menu, making this a good option for a relaxed evening meal.

88 Lounge

88 Xuan Dieu Street; tel:04 3718 8029; www.88group.vn

Set over five floors with a small front courtyard that's perfect on a warm summer's evening, 88 Lounge has an excellent wine list including numerous good options by the glass. Polished concrete, solid wooden furnishings and low lighting create a sophisticated ambiance. Live music on weekends.

Sax n Art Club, Ho Chi Minh City

Barbetta

34C Cao Ba Quat; tel: 04-3734 9134.

When Barbetta opened a few years ago it set the tone for a new wave of more innovative bars in the capital. Chock full of retro knick-knacks downstairs and with a breezy open air terrace upstairs, this is a good spot to relax over cocktails or cool beers any night of the week.

Bia Hoi Corner

Ta Hien Street, Hoan Kiem

Every evening of the week, this Old Quarter intersection is rammed with locals and tourists sitting on tiny plastic stools sipping dirt cheap *bia hoi* (fresh beer) and eating Vietnamese fast food snacks. Something of a Hanoi institution and a great place to watch the chaos of the capital's streets unfold.

CAMA ATK

73 Mai Hac De Stret, www.cama-atk.com

Open from Wed–Sat only, CAMA focusses on quality cocktails and music. Regular live performances by local and international acts.

Doors Café

11 Hang Chinh; tel: 0983029010, www.thedoorscafe.com

Dominated by a central stage, Doors Cafe is the place to head for live tunes with bands playing most nights of the week. Mix and match furnishings, friendly staff and cheap drinks.

Factory 47

40 Hang Buom; tel: 097-436 33 66

One of the most popular bars in the heart of the Old Quarter, Factory 47 is a favourite of Hanoi's younger generation and backpackers alike. With an industrial theme – think exposed pipe work and plenty of metal – this is a safe bet for a lively drink most nights of the week.

Hanoi Rock City

27 To Ngoc Van; tel: 09 1351 53 56; www.hanoirockcity.com

This is the city's largest live music and DJ venue, with regular shows by local and visiting acts. The outside area includes a small skate ramp and a small fire is often lit in the evenings making it a good spot to meet folk.

Tadioto

24 Tong Dan Street; tel: 04-2218 7200; www.tadioto.com

This is the capital's most cosmopolitan bar, frequented by the city's arty types and run by local art scene stalwart, Duc. The decor is eclectic, the cocktails second to none, and it's a good place to fall into conversation with locals, be they Vietnamese or expat.

Ho Chi Minh City

Culture

Ho Chi Minh City Conservatory of Music

112 Nguyen Du Street, District 1; tel: 08-3824 3774; www.hbso.org.vn

Founded in 1956, the conservatory is southern Vietnam's centre for classical (Western) music training, closely affiliated with the Ho Chi Minh City Ballet, Symphony, Orchestra and Opera (HBSO). Occasional classical music performances are hosted here.

Municipal Theatre

7 Lam Son Square, District 1; tel: 08-3829 9976; www.hbso.org.vn; box office: 8am–8pm performance day, otherwise Mon–Sat 8am–5.30pm; tickets: tel: 08-3925 2265

The grand Municipal Theatre (Opera House), opened in 1899 and renovated a century later, is mainly used by the Ho Chi Minh City Ballet, Symphony, Orchestra and Opera (HBSO) and visiting artists. Classical dance and music performances, including concerts, are held every month on the 9th and 19th.

Sax n' art

28 Le Loi Street, District 1; tel: 08-3822 8472; www.saxnart.com

HCMC's premier jazz and blues club is a suave, intimate venue, with black-and-white photos and vintage saxophones displayed on the walls. Live performances nightly (after 9pm), featuring well-known saxophonist-owner Tran Manh Tuan with his house band, plus occasional international guest musicians.

Yoko

22A Nguyen Thi Dieu; tel: 08 3933 0577

Live music every night from cover acts playing to big crowds of locals and expats.

If you like this, check out the Acoustic Cafe live music venue on Ngo Thoi Nhiem Street for a similar sort of night out.

Bars

Alibi

5A Nguyen Sieu Street; tel: 08-3825 6257; www.alibi.vn

A chic late night venue with cool decor and a see and be seen kind of crowd. Stays open very late making it a good after-hours whisky or cocktail option.

Blanchy's Tash

95 Hai Ba Trung Street; tel: 09-0902 8293; www.blanchystash.com

On DJ nights Blanchy's is standing room only downstairs, while the acclaimed restaurant on the same premises is well regarded for its grills.

'Beer Street'

Bui Vien Street

Saigon's answer to Hanoi's Bia Hoi Corner, Bui Vien Street comes to life after 7pm with dozens of kerb-side bars bar selling cheap bottled beer. A good place to meet other travellers and locals.

Chill Skybar

76A Le Lai Street; tel: 09-3272 0730; www.chillsaigon.com

A contender for the best open-air terrace in Saigon, Chill offers a panoramic view of the city. Cocktails are taken very seriously here by the well-heeled patrons, but it's worth checking it out if

Visit Lush in HCMC for DJs playing pop and hip hop to a mixed crowd of locals and tourists

you can take the pretension. Flip flops and shorts are not permitted and the prices will make your eyes water.

La Habana
6 Cao Ba Quat Street; tel: 08-3829 5180; www.lahabana-saigon.com
A fun night out with dancing to Latin sounds is guaranteed here. Quality cocktails and good menu of Hispanic classics.

Pasteur Street Brewing Company
144 Pasture Street; tel: 0838-239 562; www.pasturestreet.com
Pasteur Street create their own craft beers, ranging from IPAs to one of a kind concoctions using off-beat ingredients sourced in Vietnam. This location is their bar-headquarters, making it the best place to sample their latest creations.

Saigon Ranger
5/7 Nguyen Sieu Street; tel: 091-288 3006; www.facebook.com/saigonranger
Exposed brick and polished concrete create a cool space for live music at this downtown venue that's quickly established itself as a firm favourite with the city's music fans. Everything from Latin rock to experimental electro nights. Check out the website for upcoming shows.

Vasco's
74/7D Hai Ba Trung St, tel: 08-3824 2888
Still going strong after quite a few years on the Saigon scene, Vasco's has a great open air seating space out front in the courtyard which is perfect for people

watching and knocking back the happy hour cocktails.

Clubs

Apocalypse Now
2B Thi Sach Street, District 1; tel: 08-3825 6124
Saigon just has to have a club by this name. This long-running institution is by turns adored, despised and occasionally shut down. The name says it all and, like the film, you may just lose your mind here. Apocalypse plays hip dance music and features occasional live bands.

Lavish
5 Nguyen Sieu, tel: 09-3399 8389
Lavish is one of the most constantly popular clubs in the city, especially on the rammed ladies' night on Tuesdays.

Lush
2 Ly Trong Street, District 1; tel: 08-824 2496
Established by a San Francisco native, this is one of HCMC's hippest nightclubs, heaving most nights with a diverse and party-ready crowd. Lounge style sounds come from local and overseas DJs.

The Observatory
5 Nguyen tat Thanh; tel 08 3925 9415; www.facebook.com/theobservatoryhcmc
Playing host to an eclectic mix local and international DJs, the Observatory has an underground feel, a quality sound system and perhaps the best dancefloor vibe in town. Check out their Facebook page.

Vinh Nghiem Pagoda, Ho Chi Minh City

A–Z

A

Age restrictions

The age of consent in Vietnam is 18. There is not a legal drinking age minimum in Vietnam. Driving age is 15 (a Vietnamese licence is required, even for foreign visitors).

B

Budgeting

While still inexpensive for most Western travellers, Vietnam is not as cheap as it was just a few years ago. A local beer can still be found for $1 (or even less for bia hoi in Hanoi). A meal at a street vendor costs about $1, while main courses at a moderate tourist restaurant would be $5, and at a reasonably expensive restaurant $10 or $15. Basic guest-house rooms run at $10–15, rooms at moderate hotels $25–35, and resorts from $80 to several hundred. A taxi ride from the airport to downtown HCMC will average $8, while the same ride in Hanoi is around $15. Bus tickets between major cities average $7.

C

Children

Children are universally adored in Vietnam, so youngsters will be welcome almost anywhere. Most of the big cities have a water park and/or a zoo of some sort. Plus there are good beaches along the entire coast and excellent national parks to explore. Leave the buggy at home as footpaths are generally not pedestrian-friendly; a chest-mounted baby carrier is more practical. Infants and small children usually have free admission at venues.

Climate

Given Vietnam's length – it stretches 1,650km (1,000 miles) from north to south – its topography and the effect of the monsoon tropical climate, temperatures and rainfall patterns can vary widely from one region to another. In the north, temperatures can dip to as low as 10°C (50°F) and be accompanied by a biting winter wind. In the south, however, it is hot all year round.

The south has two seasons, wet and dry. During the rainy months between May and November, it rains fiercely for about 30 minutes a day (but some days not at all), normally in the afternoon or early evening. The dry season runs from December to April, with the hottest months stretching from March to late April, with temperatures well over 30°C (86°F) and with high humidity levels. Seasons are extreme along the coast between Vung Tau and Phan Rang – one of the driest spots in Southeast Asia, where it almost never rains during the dry season.

Mui Ne harbour

The north experiences four seasons. The summer months from May to September are almost always hot and humid, with the most rainfall occurring during this period. Winter, from late December to early March, is often grey, drizzly and cool.

Central Vietnam from Danang to Nha Trang has its own weather patterns due to the monsoons: the dry season is from February to September, with the most rainfall from October to December. The seasons are not as pronounced here, however, and it can rain at any time of the year, but the hottest months are June/July while the coolest months are December/January.

It's near-impossible to find a time of the year when the north, centre and south have equally good weather, but the safest bet – if you're travelling the length of Vietnam – is between March and April. The rains will have abated, humidity levels are still bearable, and it will be relatively warm and dry throughout Vietnam. However, if you are just visiting north and south Vietnam and skipping the centre, November and December are good months too.

Clothing

Bring casual, lightweight clothing in natural fabrics, which offer the most comfort in the humidity and heat. If you plan to spend time in the Highlands, then a light jacket or fleece and long trousers – especially in winter – are advisable. Rain gear, including a small umbrella, is a good idea, as it's always raining somewhere in Vietnam. Sandals or footwear that can be easily slipped off are best; shoes should be removed before entering homes and some shops.

Crime and safety

In general, Vietnam is a safe country to travel in and violent crimes against foreigners are rare. Petty theft and robbery, however, are very common. In big cities, especially Ho Chi Minh City, tourists are often the victims of pickpockets, sometimes in the form of children and women with babies, or snatch-and-grab thieves. It's not uncommon to have phones, laptops and even sunglasses snatched by passing motorcyclists.

Always leave valuables in a hotel safe; when you must carry cash, put it in a money belt worn inside your clothes. When walking or travelling in a cyclo, keep a hand firmly on bags and cameras, and on buses or trains always stay with your luggage. If you travel by train, bring a cable lock to secure your bags to your bed frame when you are sleeping.

Be careful of pavement vendors selling maps, books and souvenirs or people begging for money, especially in Hanoi and HCMC. They can easily distract you while a friend slips a hand into your pocket, grabs your wallet and vanishes. Mobile phones are easy prey, and it's not uncommon to have MP3 players, laptops and even sunglasses snatched by passing motorcyclists. Pickpockets could be children and women with babies as well.

The Vietnamese are extremely

Citadel gate, Hue

friendly and generous, but caution must be taken when making casual acquaintances. Vietnam has its fair share of con artists who hustle everything from Cambodian gems to 'genuine' bones of missing American servicemen. Beware of people who suddenly approach you in tourist areas (especially in HCMC) and engage you in conversation, or try to persuade you to go somewhere with them. This is almost always a scam.

Customs

Customs may inspect your luggage to verify that you have made a correct declaration. Currency in excess of US$7,000, and multiple electronics which look like they might be imported for resell, should be declared. Your items may be inspected to check for anything considered culturally or politically sensitive (including religious items), but this is usually only a concern for mailed parcels.

D

Disabled travellers

With all the traffic, scarcity of lifts and the sheer amount of people out and about on the streets, disabled travellers do not have an easy time in Vietnam. The roads are extremely treacherous and drivers don't tend to stop, even for the disabled, especially in the major cities. It's a contentious issue that a country with so many disabled citizens hasn't done more to accommodate them. Thankfully, it's not impossible

for adventurous disabled people with an easygoing attitude to get by. Generally the bigger hotels have wheelchair access, special toilets and lifts.

E

Electricity

The voltage in the cities and towns is generally 220V, 50 cycles. Electric sockets are standard European and/ or American, but bring an adaptor just in case. If you bring a computer to Vietnam, you should consider using a surge suppressor to protect its circuit.

Embassies and consulates

Embassies in Hanoi

Australia: 8 Dao Tan St, Ba Dinh District; tel: 04-3831 7755; www.vietnam.embassy.gov.au.

Canada: 31 Hung Vuong Street; tel: 04-3734 5000; www.dfait-maeci.gc.ca/vietnam.

New Zealand: 63 Ly Thai To Street; tel: 04-3824 1481; www.nzembassy.com.

UK: 31 Hai Ba Trung Street; tel: 04-3936 0500; www.uk-vietnam.org.

US: 7 Lang Ha Street; tel: 04-3831 4590; http://vietnam.usembassy.gov.

Consulates in Ho Chi Minh City

Australia: 5B Ton Duc Thang Street, District 1; tel: 08-3829 6035; www.hcmc.vietnam.embassy.gov.au.

Canada: 235 Dong Khoi Street, District 1; tel: 08-3827 9899.

New Zealand: 235 Dong Khoi Street,

Quang Cong Temple, Hoi An

District 1; tel: 08-3822 6907.
UK: 25 Le Duan Street, District 1; tel: 08-3829 8433; email: bcghcmc@hcm. vnn.vn.
US: 4 Le Duan Street, District 1; tel: 08-3822 9433; http://hochiminh.us consulate.gov.

Emergencies

In an emergency seek out the nearest police station – you will never be far from one in a city. The service encountered can be variable. Crimes against foreigners are taken seriously and efforts will be made to help. There are no hotlines, however. Outside of the main cities there will be little help in an emergency. Always buy travel insurance and head to Bangkok for serious medical emergencies.

Etiquette

Most meals are eaten 'family style' with shared courses. It is considered polite for hosts to occasionally dish out the best morsels into their guests' bowl throughout the meal. In many dining establishments it is common to discard table scraps on the floor or on the table itself. Observe what others do, and do likewise. Never leave chopsticks sticking upright in your bowl as it symbolises an offering to the dead.

Anyone visiting the inner sanctum of a Buddhist temple will be required to remove their shoes and hat. Temples administered by the government as 'cultural relics' (tourist attractions) generally require men to wear a shirt and trousers, and women to wear a modest top with skirt or trousers. However, such dress is not required to visit most pagodas, and Vietnamese men and women will often show up in shorts and T-shirts.

Arguing in a loud and aggressive manner will get you nowhere very fast in Vietnam. Complaining about bad service in an international-standard hotel is one thing, but such actions will fall on deaf ears at a humble guesthouse. The very notion of service is alien to the majority of the Vietnamese, and vociferous complaining won't persuade them otherwise. On the other hand, a smile can go a long way, open doors and win favours. The Vietnamese prefer a cooperative rather than confrontational approach.

As with many other parts of Asia, Confucian attitudes remain strong, and seniority demands respect whatever the circumstances. The eldest male member of any group is invariably 'in charge'. At any party it is the eldest who is served first, gets to eat first and generally dictates the course of events.

Gay and lesbian travellers

Travel in Vietnam is a relative breeze for gay people. In the last few years, HCMC's gay scene has come out in force. It's common to see Vietnamese couples at clubs and cafés downtown. Same-sex couples will not be questioned about sharing a hotel room. Pride events have grown in size in the last few years.

Front-seater cyclos are three-wheeled rickshaws pedalled by drivers

It is quite common to see open affection between Vietnamese people of the same sex in cafés or on the street. Men can often be seen holding hands, and women too, although this is usually just a sign of deep friendship. On the other hand, it is quite rare to see open affection between men and women.

Green issues

Pollution, deforestation, poaching of wildlife and sanitation are all very serious and ongoing problems. Visitors can do their part by not eating exotic animals (including those claimed to be captive-raised) or buying products made from wild animals.

Air travel produces a huge amount of carbon dioxide and is a significant contributor to global warming. If you would like to offset your flight, a number of organisations can do this for you, using online 'carbon calculators', which tell you how much you need to donate. In the UK, travellers can visit www.climatecare.org.

H

Health

Innoculations

Immunisation against hepatitis (A and B), Japanese encephalitis and tetanus are strongly encouraged. Malaria and dengue fever are prevalent throughout Vietnam, but malaria is rarely see in tourist areas. Dengue, on the other hand, is more common in both rural and urban areas. The best protection is prevention. Sleep under a mosquito net at night, use potent DEET repellent on exposed skin at all times, and where possible try to wear long-sleeved tops and trousers. Malaria-carrying mosquitoes are most active during the night, but the mosquitoes that spread dengue are most active during the day.

If you are travelling in remote areas, consult with a knowledgeable doctor to determine what anti-malarial drugs are best suited for your travels. For more information, check the website of the Centre for Disease Control (CDC) in Atlanta, United States: www.cdc.gov.

Healthcare and insurance

Healthcare in Vietnam is pay-as-you-go. Foreigners are advised to have travel insurance covering emergency evacuations.

Pharmacies and hospitals

All hospitals have 24-hour pharmacies. Private pharmacies, open late, are also common in cities.

Hanoi

Hanoi French Hospital, 1 Phuong Mai Street, Dong Da District; tel: 04-3577 1100.
Vinmec, Minh Khai Street, tel: 04 3974 3558. www.vinmec.com/

Ho Chi Minh City

Columbia Saigon, 8 Alexandre de Rhodes Street; tel: 08-3829 8520.
HCMC Family Medical Practice, Diamond Plaza, 34 Le Duan Street; tel: 08-3822 7848.

Craft workshop

I

Internet

Internet cafés with computer terminals have lost popularity with the rapid proliferation of free WiFi, and the fact that most hotels have one or two computers with free access to the internet for their guests. Most of the old internet cafés now run online games instead of providing general internet use. Most cafés, hotels and restaurants have free WiFi.

L

Language

English is now spoken in most hotels, restaurants and shops catering to tourists but learning a little of the language goes a long way. See page 134 for a handy glossary.

Left luggage

Tan Son Nhat Airport (tel: 08-3844 6665), which services Ho Chi Minh City, has left-luggage facilities (daily 7.30am–11pm) at both terminals. All hotels and guesthouses offer a left-luggage service; usually it is free, but some may levy a small daily fee for extended periods.

Lost property

Unfortunately there is very little that can be done to recover lost or stolen property in Vietnam. In the event, ask someone at your hotel to help you file a police report for insurance purposes, though police may not always be cooperative.

M

Maps

Most travel agencies offer free maps of the city in which they are located. Sinh Café Travel has a handy free booklet that includes maps for all the cities they service. Large bookstores in HCMC and Hanoi sell maps and detailed atlases for most parts of the country.

Media

All Vietnamese media, whether print, broadcast, recordings or performances, must undergo a lengthy government censorship and approval process before they go public.

Foreign newspapers and magazines can be purchased in larger bookstores in downtown HCMC and Hanoi, as well as some upscale hotels (although they aren't always current). Street vendors in tourist areas often sell second-hand copies too.

Newspapers

Vietnam has several English-language government-run newspapers, including *Viet Nam News* (www.vietnamnews. vn), *Vietnam Investment Review* (www. vir.com.vn), with its helpful weekly supplement called *Timeout* (www.vir.com. vn/client/timeout), *Vietnam Economic Times* (www.vneconomy.vn), with its weekly supplement *The Guide*, and *Viet Nam Net* (www.english.vietnamnet.vn).

Vietnamese cash

Magazines

The Word (wordvietnam.com) is the most widely available English-language lifestyle and travel magazine, aimed at an expat audience.

Radio

Two stations transmit English-language programmes on a variety of subjects several times a day on FM radio.

Television

Most hotels, restaurants, bars and cafés now have cable or satellite television with access to CNN, BBC, Australia Network, Star TV, Discovery, HBO, Cartoon Network, MTV Asia and more.

Money

Vietnam's unit of currency, the Vietnam Dong (abbreviated as VND), currently circulates in bank-notes of 500,000, 100,000, 50,000, 20,000, 10,000, 5,000, 2,000, 1,000, and 500. Notes from 10,000 to 500,000 are now made of polymer plastic, which ensures a longer life span and makes them difficult to counterfeit. The dong's value against the dollar has begun to slide in the past few years: at the time of this writing it was about VND22,000 to US$1.

Vietnamese have an obsession with unblemished US dollars and larger dong notes. They will often refuse notes with tears or writing on them, although they can usually be turned in at banks. Counterfeiting of US notes $5 and higher, as well as VND100,000 and higher, is common.

ATMs

ATM machines are now widely available in most cities. ATM fees are about US$2 per transaction at present.

Travellers' cheques and credit cards

Travellers' cheques in US dollars are accepted in most banks and in major hotels, but not in shops and not in smaller hotels or any restaurants. Major credit cards are accepted at upscale hotels, restaurants, shops and many tour offices.

Tipping and taxes

Tipping is not expected at restaurants, cafés or hotels run by Vietnamese, if they do not cater mostly to foreign tourists. However, tipping is becoming increasingly common in tourist districts. If service is good, up to 10 percent is recommended. Better hotels may impose a 10 percent tax and 5 percent service charge on receipts, although the tax isn't necessarily forwarded to the government.

Police

General police are easily identified by their olive-green uniforms with red and yellow highlights and communist emblem on their hats. Traffic police are similarly dressed in tan uniforms. 'Tour-

Phat Diem Cathedral service

ist Police' in HCMC and Hanoi are getting better but often do not speak English or have much authority. For any incidents, contact your hotel and go through local police. For serious emergencies you may wish to contact your embassy.

Post

Post offices are generally open every day from 7am to 8pm, and are the telecommunications hub of Vietnam. In the smaller towns, they often don't even identify themselves as post offices (buu dien) at all, but rather by the name of the mobile-phone plans (Vinaphone or Mobiphone) they sell. Post offices usually offer computers with internet access (although very slow), fax services, and courier services like FedEx, UPS, DHL and EMS. However, courier services are not as reliable in Vietnam as they might be in other countries. It is common for foreigners to be charged extra for some postal and courier services.

Central post offices

Hanoi: 75 Pho Dinh Tien Hoang Street; tel: 04-3825 7036 (domestic), 04-3825 2030 (international).
Ho Chi Minh City: 2 Cong Xa Paris Street; tel: 08-3829 6555.

Public holidays

1 Jan: New Year's Day
Jan/Feb: Tet
3 Feb: Founding of Vietnamese Communist Party

10th day of the third lunar month: Hung Kings Day
30 Apr: Liberation Day
1 May: International Labour Day
19 May: Ho Chi Minh's Birthday
June: Buddha's Birthday (eighth day of the fourth lunar month)
2 Sept: National Day/Independence Day

R

Religion

Vietnam is often called a Buddhist country, but this is a simplistic view. Vietnam is religiously very diverse, and most religious 'Buddhists' practice a mix of Buddhism, Confucianism, Taoism, and a heavy dose of animism and superstition. Foreigners are free to attend government-authorised temples and churches. Foreigners who visit unregistered places of worship, or churches in remote areas, may be detained and questioned by local police. Buddhists and Catholics will have no difficulty finding convenient places of worship. Most large towns have at least one Protestant and one Catholic church each. HCMC also has several mosques, Hindu temples, and at least one Chabad Lubavitch (Jewish centre).

S

Smoking

Smoking is not only common, it is almost expected of all men. It is gener-

ally considered unfeminine for women to smoke, though today more and more do.

T

Telephones

When calling a city in Vietnam from overseas, dial the country code 84, followed by the area code but drop the prefix zero. When making a domestic call from one province or city to another in Vietnam, dial the area code first (including the prefix zero). Note: local calls within the same province/city do not require the area code.

Area codes
Binh Thuan (Phan Thiet) 062
Lam Dong (Da Lat) 063
Ninh Thuan (Phan Rang) 068
Can Tho 0710
Dak Lak (Buon Ma Thuot) 0500
Danang 0511
HCMC 08
Hanoi 04
Khanh Hoa (Nha Trang) 058
Lao Cai (Sa Pa) 020
Quang Nam (Hoi An) 0510
Quang Ninh 033
Tay Ninh 066
Thua Thien-Hue 054
Vinh Long 070

Country codes
Australia 0061
Canada 001
Ireland 00353
UK 0044
USA 001

Mobile phones
Most mobile phone users from overseas who have signed up for roaming facility with their service providers back home will be able to hook up with the network that Vietnam uses. Alternatively, cheap prepaid SIM cards can be purchased in Vietnam very cheaply and phone credit can be bought on almost every street.

Time zones

Vietnam is seven hours ahead of GMT. It does not observe daylight-saving time.

Toilets

Most bus trips that cater to foreign tourists include scheduled stops at places that have basic Western-style toilets. Shopping centres, most hotels and the better restaurants and cafés also normally have Western-style toilet facilities. However, go off the beaten tourist track and you're likely to encounter squat toilets. Be sure to carry a pack of tissue paper, as it is unlikely to be available in these situations.

Tourist information

Vietnam's tourism industry lags behind other Asian countries (and for some travellers this may be a good thing). The official representative for Vietnam's tourism – domestically as well as overseas – comes under the purview of the government-operated Vietnam National

Refuelling a Vietnam Airlines plane

Administration of Tourism (VNAT; www.
vietnamtourism.com). However, it is
more involved in the construction of
new hotels and infrastructure development than in providing tourist services.
State-run 'tourist offices' under the
VNAT are merely tour agents and are not
geared towards meeting the require-
ments of most travellers.

Transport

Airports and arrival

The main international airports are in
Ho Chi Minh City (HCMC), Hanoi and
Danang. HCMC is the main gateway to
the country; fewer international flights
go to Hanoi. Danang receives international flights from Singapore, Bangkok
and Hong Kong.

Hanoi

Noi Bai International Airport is located
about 25km north of downtown Hanoi
via an excellent new road and the
impressive Cau Nhat Tan Bridge. It is
served by domestic flights as well as
international services from Europe,
Australia and Asia. For flight information, call Operation Control Centre, tel:
04-3827 1513.

Cover the distance from Noi Bai International Airport to downtown Hanoi in
an airport taxi, ranks of which wait outside arrivals and run on a meter.

Ho Chi Minh City

HCMC's Tan Son Nhat International Airport – just 7km (4 miles) from the city

centre – is Vietnam's busiest airport
hub, with nearly two-thirds of international arrivals and departures into
Vietnam using it. For flight information,
call the Operation Control Centre, tel:
08-3844 6662/08-3848 5383.

Although Tan Son Nhat International
Airport is only 7km (4 miles) northwest of
the centre, the ride into town can take up
to 30 or 40 minutes. The best option is
an airport taxi. There are no pre-arranged
fixed rates, instead taxis are metered
and you will be given a paper listing the
number of your taxi before you depart.

Danang

Danang International Airport, the main
hub that serves central Vietnam, is
located a few kilometres from the city
centre. The number of direct international flights is growing rapidly. For flight
information call 0511-382 3377. From
Danang, places like Hoi An and Hue are
easily accessible by road.

By road

It is possible to enter Vietnam from
China at the Lang Son and Lao Cai
border crossings in the north. A few
travellers travel overland from Laos to
Vietnam by bus via the Lao Bao border
crossing in central Vietnam. Although
definitely not common practice, it
is becoming more popular among
budget travellers. Travellers also can
enter Vietnam by crossing the border
with Cambodia at Moc Bai, only a few
hours by road from HCMC, or at Vinh

Xuong, located about 30km (18 miles) north of Chau Doc in south Vietnam. Numerous other small border crossings exist.

Public transport

Vietnam lacks a well-developed public transport system. The best options are the train system or the private open-tour bus companies. However, in a few years, Hanoi will have a sky train system and HCMC will have an underground network.

By train

Train travel, operated by Vietnam Railways (www.vr.com.vn) in Vietnam, is very slow. Due to the existence of just a single track along the coast, train travel in Vietnam is subject to frequent delays. The fastest express train from Hanoi to HCMC (called the Reunification Express), the SE4 covers 1,730km (1,073 miles) in 29 hours, with the slower ones (like the TBN) taking up to 41 hours because of the numerous stops they make. There are five classes of train travel in Vietnam: hard seat, soft seat, hard sleeper, soft sleeper and soft sleeper with air conditioning – this last option available only on certain trains.

Hanoi's railway station is at 120 Le Duan Street; tel: 04-3942 3697 (located at the far western end of Tran Hung Dao Street). The ticket office is open daily from 7.30–11.30am and 1.30–3.30pm.

Trains leave HCMC for the northern coastal towns from the railway station, which is located at 1 Nguyen Thong Street, District 3 (tel: 08-3843 6528). The ticket office is open daily 7.15am to 11am and 1pm to 3pm.

By bus

If you are planning to travel long distance by bus, it is best to use one of the comfortable 'Open Tour' air-conditioned bus services. Departing every day, the bus allows you to you to get on or off anywhere along the route from either Hanoi or HCMC (like Hue, Hoi An, Danang, Nha Trang, Da Lat and Mui Ne) with few restrictions. The buses make stops every couple of hours for food and toilet breaks.

Taxis

There are many taxi companies servicing the major cities and they are far better now than in the past. Stick to the bigger brand names below:

Hanoi: Hanoi Taxi, tel: 04-3853 5353; CP Taxi, tel: 04-3826 2626; ABC Taxi, tel: 04-3719 1919; Mai Linh Taxi, tel: 04-3822 2555.

Ho Chi Minh City: Mai Linh tel: 08-3822 2666; Saigon Tourist, tel: 08-3845 8888; Vina Taxi, tel: 08-3811 1111; Vinasun, tel: 08-3827 2727.

Driving

By law, all foreign drivers must possess a Vietnamese driver's licence, which can take more than a month to acquire,

Truong Tien Bridge, Hue

thus ruling out driving for most foreign visitors. This said, many tourists do rent motorbikes, though traffic police in the cities have been known to check drivers' licences and confiscate motorbikes.

It is also possible to hire a vehicle with driver, easily done at tourist offices or agencies which arrange tours. Check what costs are included and your liability carefully and ensure all involved have signed a contract including your planned itinerary.

Visas and passports

Visa regulations were in the process of being relaxed at the time of print, with nationals of several European nations including the UK exempted from visas for stays of two weeks. Check the Vietnamese Ministry of Foreign Affairs website at www.mofa.gov.vn for up-to-date information.

Otherwise, getting a visa is fairly straightforward. The best way is to apply for a visa letter prior to your arrival. This can be done online via many travel agents in Vietnam. You will then be able to get your visa on arrival at international airports. Those travelling overland will need to arrange their visa in advance via a Vietnamese embassy.

The easy way of getting a visa is to use a travel agent. There will be a commission charge on top of the usual visa processing fee paid to the Vietnamese Embassy or Consulate. In addition to the application form, visitors must submit a valid passport and two passport-size photos. Allow 5–7 working days for approval. Individual travellers may also apply for a visa directly with the Vietnamese Embassy or Consulate in their home country. For a list of Vietnamese foreign missions overseas, check the Ministry of Foreign Affairs website. Visas are issued for one or three months and for single or multiple entry. The visa fee changes fairly regularly so check for the current price with your agent or embassy.

W

Websites

Vietnam National Administration of Tourism (www.vietnamtourism.com)
Ministry of Foreign Affairs (www.mofa.gov.vn/en)
Local organisation combating the illegal wildlife trade (www.envietnam.org)
Tourism office for Da Lat (www.dalattourist.com.vn)
Tourism site of Halong Bay (www.halong.org.vn)
Government and tourism site for Hanoi (www.hanoi.gov.vn)
HCMC's Department of Tourism (http://tourism.hochiminhcity.gov.vn)
Tourism information in and around Mui Ne Beach (www.muinebeach.net)
Khanh Hoa Province Culture, Sport and Tourism Authority (http://nhatrang-travel.com)

LANGUAGE

Vietnamese (tieng Viet) is the nation's official language. It is spoken by practically the entire population, although with marked variations in pronunciation and some differences in vocabulary between North, Center and South. Vietnamese belongs to the Mon-Khmer branch of the Austroasiatic language family. Around 60 percent of Vietnamese words have their roots in the Chinese language, the result of over a thousand years of Chinese colonisation and cultural transfer. Courtly Vietnamese was written using standard Chinese characters until the arrival of the French in the 19th century, but the development of a demotic writing system (Chu Nôm) in the 13th century allowed the expression of a uniquely Vietnamese literary identity. Western missionaries, most notably Alexandre de Rhodes in the 17th century, developed a Romanized script for Vietnamese, which was formalized by French linguists into the present day Quoc Ngu (national language).

Ironically, the explosion of literacy this enabled was a key factor in the development of Vietnamese national consciousness, which ultimately led to the Vietnamese revolution. Chinese, Khmer, Hmong, Chăm and many other languages are also widely spoken in Vietnam, a reflection of the historical patterns of colonisation and migration that have formed the modern nation. Vietnamese continues to evolve, invent-ing terms for new technologies and con-cepts, and borrowing voraciously from English, Japanese and Korean as it once did from Chinese and French.

Pronunciation

While the Romanized writing system is a boon for the student of Vietnamese, the language is notoriously difficult to pro-nounce. Tones and the different vowel pronunciations are indicted by diacritics written above and below the words. The best way to tackle the language's tricky pronunciation is to ask a native speaker to repeat the word in question until the listener feels they can replicate the tone. Most Vietnamese people are remarka-bly patient and supportive of foreigners attempting to speak their language.

As for other languages, you will have to look hard to find people who speak French, although in parts of Vietnam (especially Nha Trang) Russian is having a resurgence. English is spoken in well touristed locations, and English speak-ers will discover loan words such as 'cool' peppering contemporary Vietnamese.

Greetings

The Vietnamese word for hello, 'chào', sounds fortuitously like the Italian 'ciao'. Overseas visitors will often be greeted with the polite form 'xin chào', or even the English-influenced con-struction 'chào buoi sáng' (good morn-

Speak to the locals in Phat Diem

ing). In normal usage, 'chào' is followed by a personal pronoun appropriate to the age, gender and status of the person being addressed. Thus:

for a lady the age of your grandmother *Chào bà.*

for a lady the age of your aunt *chào co*

for a lady slightly older than you *chào chi*

for a man the age of your grandfather *chào ông*

for a man slightly older than you *chào anh*

for a man the age of your uncle *chào bác*

for a person the age of your younger sibling *chào em*

for a child *chào con*

Goodbye *Tam biet*

Excuse me (begging pardon) *Xin loi*

Excuse me (asking for service) *Chi ii! Anh ii! Em ii! (etc)*

Thank you *Cam in*

Yes *Da, vâng*

No *Không*

No thanks (polite) *Da không, không a*

I (to an equal) *tôi*

I (to someone the age of your younger sibling) *Anh, Chi*

I (to someone the age of an aunt, uncle or grandparent) *Cháu*

I (to someone the age of an elder sibling) *em*

Useful phrases

How much does it cost? *Bao nhiêu tien?*

Bill/check please! *Xin tính tien!*

Where is... (the post office)? *(Buu dien)... o dau?*

Just looking (not shopping) *không mua*

I don't want it *không muon*

I don't want to buy it *không mua, không mua đâu!*

I want... *Tôi muon...*

Have you eaten? *Ăn com chua?*

My name is... *Tôi tên là...*

What's your name? *Tên (em/anh/chi) là gì?*

How are you? *Khoe không ?*

Fine thank you *Khoe, da khoe*

Don't worry about it *không sao đâu*

Where are you from? *Ban là nguoi nuoc nào?*

I am from Australia. *Tôi là nguoi Úc.*

Numbers

0 *không*
1 *mot*
2 *hai*
3 *ba*
4 *bón*
5 *năm*
6 *sáu*
7 *bay*
8 *tám*
9 *chính*
10 *muoi*
11 *muoi mot*
12 *muoi hai*
13 *muoi ba*
20 *hai muoi*
30 *ba muoi*
100 *uot trăm*
1,000 *mot nghin*
1,000,000 *mot triu*

BOOKS AND FILM

Vietnam's cinematic identity has been defined internationally by foreign-made war or Indochina-set films. Nationally, the state-run, domestic film industry has produced low-budget, nationalistic-themed films for decades. Since 2002, however, the government has eased control, resulting in greater creative freedom and a flourishing commercial industry – the majority based in HCMC. Armed with cash and expertise, overseas Vietnamese directors are increasingly involved in Vietnam's film industry, creating internationally acclaimed films.

Classical Vietnamese literature concerns itself greatly with myths and legends. Undoubtedly the best-known piece of writing in Vietnam is *Tale of Kieu*, a 3,254-verse epic poem written by 18th-century author Nguyen Du. Not surprisingly, war and colonial rule dominate literature; inevitably, the Vietnam War and its aftermath receive most coverage, with countless books dissecting this era. Government censorship has resulted in this genre being flooded by foreign authors rather than locals, although some of the best 20th-century Vietnamese literature has been written by Vietnamese living abroad.

Films

Apocalypse Now (1979) Perhaps the most famous and highly regarded of all the Vietnam war movies.

The Buffalo Boy (2004) This excellent film by Minh Nguyen Vo tells the coming-of-age story of Kim, 15, who sets off with his family's two buffalo in search of grass during the rainy season.

Bi, dung so! (2010) Shot in Hanoi, this modern classic focussed on 6 year old Bi and his dysfunctional family.

Cyclo (1995) Directed by Tran Anh Hung, the film follows a brother and sister who are forced into working for a criminal gang after the brother loses his cyclo.

The Deer Hunter (1978) A ground-breaking combat epic.

Green Berets (1968) John Wayne's anti-communist feature.

De Mai Tinh 2 (2014) This slapstick comedy that broke local box-office records was not without controversy, with some LGBT campaigners protesting against its flamboyantly camp central character.

Full Metal Jacket (1987) A hard hitting film shot largely in London's docklands.

The Quiet American (2002) This film adaptation of Graham Greene's novel won government approval for filming almost entirely in Vietnam.

The Scent Of Green Papaya (1993) French-Vietnamese director Tran Anh Hung's film is a nostalgic look at pre-war Saigon and the first Vietnamese film nominated for an Academy Award.

Three Seasons (1998) Vietnamese-Californian director Tony Bui's acclaimed 1998 film was shot in and around

HCMC, with a cast including street kids.
The White Silk Dress (2007) This award-winning Vietnamese war-drama epic was directed by Luu Huynh and cost over US$2 million, making it one of the most expensive Vietnamese films ever made. The story follows a poor mother and father determined to ensure their children have the best chances in life.

Books

Fiction

A Vietcong Memoir, Truong Nhu Tang (1985). The voyage of a scion of the Saigon bourgeoisie to the jungle, to the National Liberation Front, to victory and finally to escape as a boat person.

The Tale of Kieu, Huynh Sanh Thong (1987). An English translation of the famed epic poem, about a beautiful young woman whose life goes terribly wrong.

The Sorrow of War, Bao Ninh (1995). This North Vietnam war veteran wrote one of the first and best war novels from a northern soldier's perspective.

Dumb Luck: A Novel , Vu Trong Phung (2002). This is a translation of a hilarious tongue-in-cheek satire of Hanoians in the 1930s.

The Quiet American, Graham Greene (1955). Written in the the Hotel Continental, this novel is set at the height of Vietnam's anti-colonial fight and foretells American involvement in Vietnam.

The Lover, Marguerite Duras (1984). The author was born near Saigon in 1914, but left for France aged 17. Her best-selling autobiographical novel tells the story of a clandestine affair between a French teenage girl and a wealthy Chinese man from Cholon.

Vietnam, as if..., Kim Huynh (2015). This book follows five young people who have moved from the countryside to the city, their everyday lives illuminating the most pressing issues in Vietnam today.

Non–fiction

A Dragon Apparent, Norman Lewis (1951). Indochina travels in the twilight of the French Empire.

All the Wrong Places by James Fenton (1988). This English poet-journalist was on the tank that crashed through the Independence Palace gates on 30 April 1975; this work details his first-hand account of Saigon's liberation.

Dispatches (1977) Michael Herr. One of several journalists who lived at the HCMC Caravelle Hotel, these are Herr's candid war memoirs.

Fire in the Lake, Frances FitzGerald (1972). A Pulitzer Prize-winning classic on the Vietnam War.

Ho Chi Minh: A Life, William Duiker (2001). An excellent biography of revolutionary and political leader Ho Chi Minh.

From a Chinese City (1957). Gontran de Poncins A French ethnographer, Gontran de Poncins vividly captures 1950s Cholon through detailing his stay there in 1955.

Vietnam, Now, David Lamb (2003). A journalist in the south from 1969 to 1975, Lamb returned to Vietnam in 1999 to open an office for the *LA Times*.

ABOUT THIS BOOK

This *Explore Guide* has been produced by the editors of Insight Guides, whose books have set the standard for visual travel guides since 1970. With top-quality photography and authoritative recommendations, these guidebooks bring you the very best routes and itineraries in the world's most exciting destinations.

BEST ROUTES

The routes in the book provide something to suit all budgets, tastes and trip lengths. As well as covering the destination's many classic attractions, the itineraries track lesser-known sights. The routes embrace a range of interests, so whether you are an art fan, a gourmet, a history buff or have kids to entertain, you will find an option to suit.

We recommend reading the whole of a route before setting out. This should help you to familiarise yourself with it and enable you to plan where to stop for refreshments – options are shown in the 'Food and Drink' box at the end of each tour.

For our pick of the tours by theme, consult Recommended Routes for… (see pages 6–7).

INTRODUCTION

The routes are set in context by this introductory section, giving an overview of the destination to set the scene, plus background information on food and drink, shopping and more, while a succinct history timeline highlights the key events over the centuries.

DIRECTORY

Also supporting the routes is a Directory chapter, with a clearly organised A–Z of practical information, our pick of where to stay while you are there and select restaurant listings; these eateries complement the more low-key cafés and restaurants that feature within the routes and are intended to offer a wider choice for evening dining. Also included here are some nightlife listings, plus a handy language guide and our recommendations for books and films about the destination.

ABOUT THE AUTHORS

David Lloyd has contributed to and authored numerous guidebooks, in addition to his work as a photographer; his images have been published in titles including the *New York Times*. Alongside this, he runs bespoke tours and is co-founder of Velo Vietnam, providing road cycling experiences throughout the country.

Adam Bray has contributed to nearly 20 guidebooks on Vietnam and neighbouring countries in Southeast Asia, including several for Insight Guides. He is a specialist in minority cultures, present and past, and has uncovered a number of ancient Cham temple ruins in his home province.

Some of the tours in this book were originally conceived by Samantha Coomber and Lucy Forwood.

CONTACT THE EDITORS

We hope you find this Explore Guide useful, interesting and a pleasure to read. If you have any questions or feedback on the text, pictures or maps, please do let us know. If you have noticed any errors or outdated facts, or have suggestions for places to include on the routes, we would be delighted to hear from you. Please drop us an email at hello@insightguides.com. Thanks!

CREDITS

Explore Vietnam
Editor: Sarah Clark
Author: David Lloyd, Adam Bray
Head of Production: Rebeka Davies
Picture Editor: Tom Smyth
Cartography: original cartography Lovell Johns, updated by Carte
Photo credits: Alamy 137; Corbis 27; Getty Images 26, 60/61, 100/101T; Hilton Hotels & Resorts 104; iStock 25; Leonardo 100MR, 100ML, 105, 106, 107; Peter Stuckings/Apa Publications 1, 4ML, 4MC, 4MR, 4MR, 4MC, 4ML, 4/5T, 6TL, 6MC, 6ML, 6BC, 7T, 7MR, 7M, 7MR, 8ML, 8MC, 8ML, 8MC, 8MR, 8MR, 8/9T, 10, 11, 12, 13, 14, 15L, 14/15, 16, 17, 18, 19L, 18/19, 20/21, 22, 23, 24, 28ML, 28MC, 28MR, 28ML, 28MC, 28MR, 28/29T, 30, 31, 32, 33L, 32/33, 34, 35, 36, 37L, 36/37, 38, 39, 40, 41L, 40/41, 42, 43, 44, 45, 46, 47L, 46/47, 48, 49, 50, 51, 52, 53L, 52/53, 54, 55L, 54/55, 56, 57, 58, 59L, 58/59, 62, 63L, 62/63, 64, 65, 66, 67L, 66/67, 68, 69, 70, 71L, 70/71, 72/73, 74, 75, 76, 77, 78, 79L, 78/79, 80, 81, 82, 83, 84, 85, 86, 87L, 86/87, 88, 89, 90/91, 92, 93, 94, 95L, 94/95, 96, 97L, 96/97, 98, 99, 100ML, 100MC, 100MR, 100MC, 102/103, 110, 111, 112, 113, 114, 115, 116/117, 118, 119, 120/121, 122, 123, 124, 125, 126, 127, 128, 129, 130/131, 132, 133, 134/135; Photoshot 136; Six Senses 108; Victoria Hotels & Resorts 109
Cover credits: Shutterstock (main and BL)

Printed by CTPS – China

Every effort has been made to provide accurate information in this publication, but changes are inevitable. The publisher cannot be responsible for any resulting loss, inconvenience or injury.

DISTRIBUTION

UK, Ireland and Europe
Apa Publications (UK) Ltd
sales@insightguides.com
United States and Canada
Ingram Publisher Services
ips@ingramcontent.com
Southeast Asia
Woodslane
info@woodslane.com.au
Australia and New Zealand
Apa Publications (Singapore) Pte
singaporeoffice@insightguides.com
Hong Kong, Taiwan and China
Apa Publications (HK) Ltd
hongkongoffice@insightguides.com
Worldwide
Apa Publications (UK) Ltd
sales@insightguides.com

SPECIAL SALES, CONTENT LICENSING AND COPUBLISHING

Insight Guides can be purchased in bulk quantities at discounted prices. We can create special editions, personalised jackets and corporate imprints tailored to your needs.
sales@insightguides.com
www.insightguides.biz

INDEX

MAP LEGEND

- ● Start of tour
- ⟶ Tour & route direction
- ❶ Recommended sight
- ❷ Recommended restaurant/café
- ★ Place of interest
- ❶ Tourist information
- ✉ Main post office
- 𝟙 Statue/monument
- 𝚰 Tower
- ᴍ Museum/gallery
- 📖 Library
- 🎭 Theatre
- 📡 Radio mast
- ⛴ Pedestrian ferry
- ═══ Railway
- ═══ Motorway
- ---- Ferry route
- 🚌 Main bus station
- 🚠 Cable car
- ✈ Airport international
- ✈ Airport regional
- 🗼 Lighthouse
- ⚓ Beach
- 🏞 Cave
- ▲ Summit
- ☀ Viewpoint
- ⋮ Ancient Site
- ✚ Cathedral/church
- ▬ ▪ ▬ National boundary
- ·──·── County boundary
-     Important building
-     Hotel
-     Shopping /market
-     Park
-     Pedestrian area
-     Urban area
-     Non-urban area
-     National park
-     Marsh

INSIGHTGUIDES.COM

The Insight Guides website offers a unique way to plan and book tailor-made trips online. Be inspired by our curated destination content, read our daily travel blog and build your own dream trip from our range of customisable experiences, created by our local experts.

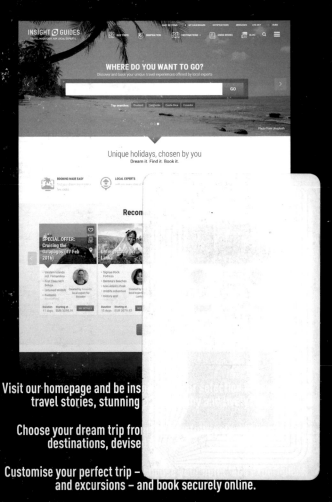

Visit our homepage and be ins
travel stories, stunning

Choose your dream trip from
destinations, devise

Customise your perfect trip –
and excursions – and book securely online.

INSIGHT ⊙ GUIDES

TRAVEL MADE EASY. ASK LOCAL EXPERTS.